"A few years ago, I had the pleasure of visiting Miriam (and Paul) at their Wildflower farm in Coldwater Ontario. In good company with numerous birds, butterflies, bees and countless pollinators, we strolled through fields of Liatris, Echinacea, Rudbeckia and many other incredible native plants. It is an experience that I will not soon forget. To know that Miriam has now put both her passion and many years of hands-on experience into words in her upcoming new book is very exciting indeed!"

– *Paul Zammit, Director of Horticulture, Toronto Botanical Garden*

"Miriam Goldberger has devoted a lifetime of work to propagating native plants and advocating for their widespread horticultural use. Through Wildflower Farm, she has not only made North American native plants widely available, but also educated gardeners about which plants grow best in which environments and why native plants are integral to the success of healthy ecosystems. *Taming Wildflowers* promises to build on her important legacy and continue to inspire others to share in her love of our native flora."

– *Mark Richardson, Director of Horticulture, New England Wild Flower Society*

"Miriam Goldberger's mission is to encourage as many people as possible to grow, design, decorate, arrange and love the flowers that have inspired her passion. It's easy to get gardeners to welcome native plants to their own backyards – they sell themselves with their beauty, sustainability and as vital constituents of our local ecosystems."

– *Ken Druse, author of* Natural Companions: the Garden Lover's Guide to Plant Combinations, *and other books on eco-sensitive gardening*

"I have known Miriam through her work in the business of wildflowers for about 20 years. I have grown to admire her passion for wildflowers and the depth of her knowledge of this fascinating topic. She has achieved a level of awareness about the benefits of native plants that is unprecedented."

– *Mark Cullen, Canada's gardening guru; multi-book author and host of HGTV Canada's "Mark Cullen Gardening"*

"Miriam Goldberger has long been the prime voice for wildflowers and how they make the ecosystem hum. Now she's written a book about her wildly floriferous passion, filled with fresh photographs of wildflower gardens and bouquets. *Taming Wildflowers* will inspire anyone who loves these amazing and intricate plants and will entice a new generation of gardeners to fall in love with wildflowers."

– *Marjorie Harris, author of* Botanica North America *and* Ecological Gardening

taming wildflowers

BRINGING THE BEAUTY AND SPLENDOR OF NATURE'S BLOOMS INTO YOUR OWN BACKYARD

taming wildflowers

BRINGING THE BEAUTY AND SPLENDOR OF NATURE'S BLOOMS INTO YOUR OWN BACKYARD

MIRIAM GOLDBERGER

PITTSBURGH

Taming Wildflowers
Bringing the Beauty and Splendor of Nature's Blooms into Your Own Backyard

ISBN-13: 978-0-9855622-6-7

Library of Congress Control Number: 2013941488
CIP information available upon request

First Edition, 2014

St. Lynn's Press . POB 18680 . Pittsburgh, PA 15236
412.466.0790 . www.stlynnspress.com

Book design–Holly Rosborough
Editor–Catherine Dees
Editorial interns–Allison Keene, Claire Stetzer

Photo credits:
Courtney Lee: page 175 (Anne and Nick; Anne and her bridesmaids); Douglas Fisher: page 4
Emily Santi: pages 174, 176 (bridesmaids bouquets); Jocelyn Shipticki: pages 22, 177 (top photos)
Marette Sharp: pages 18, 27, 134, 135, 139, 141, 142, 161, 164 (earthy colors); Marielle Anzelone: 150; Maria Levitov: page 17;
Paul Jenkins: many seedling and flower photos in Chapter 3; Natasha McFayden: page 168;
Nikki Heseltine: page 173 (two left photos and top right photo); Yvonne Cunnington: pages 149, 151 (meadow)

Wedding Album photo credits: Harvest: Miriam Goldberger; Design Workshop: Miriam Goldberger;
Chantelle Wedding: all by Nikki Heseltine (except the bottom middle photo – Miriam Goldberger); Katrina Wedding:
all by Emily Santi; Anne Wedding: all Courtney Lee (except the top middle and right photos – Miriam Goldberger)
All other photos by the author.

page 13, Illustration "Parts of a Flower" reprinted by permission of the AIMS Education Foundation;
from The Budding Botanist ©2009 AIMS Education Foundation. All rights reserved. www.aimsedu.org

Printed in Canada
on certified FSC recycled paper using soy-based inks

This title and all of St. Lynn's Press books may be purchased for educational, business or sales promotional use.
For information please write:
Special Markets Department . St. Lynn's Press . POB 18680 . Pittsburgh, PA 15236

10 9 8 7 6 5 4 3 2 1

To my ever-patient partner in life,

love and flower farming.

There may be no such thing as too many flowers,

but in this wide wide world

there is only one Paul Jenkins.

Table of Contents

Introduction – How Wildflowers Changed My World (a love story) ix

Chapter 1 – Wildflowers and Us: a beautiful, symbiotic relationship 1

Chapter 2 – Up Close and Personal with Pollinators 11

Chapter 3 – The Wildflowers 29

Chapter 4 – Non-Native Must Haves 109

Chapter 5 – Making Babies 129

Chapter 6 – Get in the Garden! 145

Chapter 7 – Your Wildflower Design Studio 159

Chapter 8 – The DIY Wildflower Wedding Experience 171

Last Words 187

Appendices
Index – Wildflowers and Native Grasses 189
Best Wildflowers/Native Grasses by Soil Type 190

Acknowledgments 192

About the Author 194

How Wildflowers Changed My World

I love all flowers, but to me, wildflowers are the ultimate expression of floral perfection. They are nature's flawless plan for pollination and they never fail to impress me with their flat-out beauty.

*　*　*

No Such Thing as Too Many Flowers

For as long as we humans have been stumbling around on the planet, we've been drawn to wild-flowers. For the past 30 years I have been thoroughly addicted to the colorful, magical creatures we call wildflowers. And you are too! Yes, you! (Forgive me for pointing.) Right now you're flipping through the pages of this book, hungry for the pictures. I venture to say, you know EXACTLY what I mean.

I fell in love with flowers long before I realized that they would define and illuminate my world. I was certainly not present and accounted for during high school biology class when we trudged through the chapter on flower anatomy. I had zero interest in charts, graphs, excruciatingly detailed science reports or the memorization of scientific terms. Latin? You've got to be kidding.

What did catch my attention in class were the cool shapes, colors and textures of leaves and flowers. Studying plants transported me back to my tomboy days – the hours I spent hiding out in my apple-tree fort behind the garage, staring up into the canopy of green leaves and inhaling the heady aroma of white apple blossoms in the spring.

I fell in love with flowers because they are just so amazing to look at and be around. I can lose myself in the vortex of their playful spirals; I'm a sucker for their colors and textures. They calm me and bring me unspeakable joy.

My mother gardened avidly, but only indoors. Lemon trees graced the gas fireplace in our dining room. African violets near the kitchen table greeted me each morning over toast and orange juice. Legions of spider plants hung merrily from every kitchen window. (This was the early '60s, when striped spider plants were all the rage.) My mother's indoor-plant passion blossomed into an active membership in the New Jersey Cactus Society and then exploded into a greenhouse extension off the kitchen. Years later, my own young family (somehow) managed to successfully avoid massive barrel cactus stabbings while visiting Grandma's greenhouse – with three active kids under the age of six, no less.

In addition to her flair for floral design, my mother was a collector of floral art. In hindsight,

my daily exposure to this artwork was an obvious indicator that I was destined, programmed, nurtured – cultivated, if you will – to fall in love with flowers.

When my mother first acquired this painting it lived in an intimate corner of the kitchen greenhouse, above several huge cactuses. Near the end of her years, dementia made it nearly impossible for her to communicate verbally. Yet, each time we visited, no matter how disoriented she was, she would draw my attention to that painting, and without fail, summon the will and the words to remind me, "Don't forget! When I die, this painting is yours."

There has never been a time in human history when flowers were not drawn, painted or picked. No matter who you are or where you live, there has surely been a time when flowers lifted your spirits and stirred the strings of your soul.

It wasn't until 1982 that I reconnected with flowers. Until that time, my life revolved around pregnancy and childbirth. I was the founder and director of Preggae Woman, a prenatal and postpartum fitness program in Toronto. I'd studied dance all my life, and after graduating from college with a BA in dance, I was drawn into the field of childbirth and midwifery. Gardening was not on my radar.

And then...

One day, on a whim, I bought some zinnia seeds at a local grocery store. I remember carefully placing the tiny pots of planted seeds on top of my funky turquoise refrigerator and anxiously checking the soil, waiting for something – anything – to happen.

Finally, a few days later a tiny, light green cotyledon poked its head through the soil.

I worked at home so I had the luxury of obsessively checking my project. I was mesmerized watching the hour-by-hour changes my seedlings were undergoing: from the first glint of green pushing up through the brown dirt to the unfurling of the second set of leaves. A tiny magical kingdom emerged before my eyes. It was the coolest thing I had ever seen…and I was hooked. But I was nowhere near doing it on a larger scale. That happened a little later, on a morning when my partner, Paul, and I were browsing through the classified ads (always a dangerous thing to do when there's an idea germinating in the back of your mind).

We noticed a farm for rent just outside the city. Out of just plain curiosity we went to see it. That was all it took. We'd always dreamed of trying country life on for size.

Before I knew it, Paul and I, our two little boys and 5-week-old daughter had a 100-acre flower farm and we were growing plants in earnest. Very quickly, we outfitted our grungy farm basement with a collection of recycled fluorescent fixtures with grow lights, and we were producing hundreds of plants each spring. But what a chore it was to drag the heavy trays up and down the steep stairs to harden off the young plants. We longed for the luxury and efficiency a greenhouse would bring.

A few years later, when we decided to marry, instead of a bridal registry, we asked wedding guests to contribute to our greenhouse fund. They generously obliged and shortly after the wedding

we constructed our first 20 x 60 greenhouse. The following spring I grew thousands of flowers. I felt utterly compelled to grow every kind of flower available in the seed catalogues, and so we did. Now I had acres of flowers to tend; I loved every hard-working minute of it. We soon became Canada's first pick-your-own flower farm. We named our floriferous paradise Wildflower Farm, not because we were actually growing wildflowers yet, but because we loved the romantic notion of them. That was about to change.

I'd converted a small animal barn into an unconventional shop with display beds in front and I needed to find some super-low-maintenance plants for them. So I began experimenting with hardy, perennial wildflowers and native grasses. Wildflowers! Where had you been all my life? And, oh, the butterflies and the songbirds that came with them! Why weren't these gorgeous creatures growing in every garden? I couldn't get over how easy native plants were to grow and maintain, how long-lived they were and, most of all, how utterly beautiful they were. Plus, contrary to popular belief, they made stunning bouquets. You might say they ticked all my boxes of what flowers should be. My personal motto became: There is no such thing as too many flowers.

When my husband and I started growing wild-flowers and native grasses, the local farmers thought it was pretty darn funny to see the city slickers (now referred to as "citiots") growing weeds. They aren't laughing anymore.

* * *

This book celebrates the beauty of wildflowers, but there is so much more to them that I want to tell you about. They are masters (mistresses?) of erosion control, soils engineering, water management, polli-nator-enticement, climate adaptability, ecosystem coordination, carbon sequestration, habitat protec-tion – and that's just a start. They are rugged beau-ties that ask for little and just keep giving.

It's well past time that we turn the spotlight on them and realize their incredible gifts to us and to the whole of life around us. As happens too often in our history, we humans don't fully appreciate the value of something until we're about to lose it. Today, we are perilously close to losing the presence of wildflowers in North America; and in losing them we face the loss of the vital pollinators responsible for the great majority of our food crops. As we're learning more and more, everything in nature is intricately connected to everything else.

What can you do to help? Plant wildflowers, of course! Not only are they lovely, they provide the essential nutrition needed by our beloved beneficial wildlife. I'm so happy to be part of the solution to this dire ecological problem, and privileged to live among the wildflowers each and every day. For me,

they signify the emotional connection between the earth and nature – a celebration of life, optimism and overcoming adversity.

I invite you to come along with me as we explore the profoundly beautiful world of wildflowers. 🦌

Miriam

ONE

Wildflowers and Us:
a Beautiful, Symbiotic Relationship

*Flowers changed the face of the planet. Without them, the world we know –
even man himself – would never have existed... Today we know that
the appearance of the flowers contained also the equally
mystifying emergence of man.*

– LOREN EISELEY, *"HOW FLOWERS CHANGED THE WORLD"*

The great modern naturalist, Loren Eiseley, recognized the interlinked complexity of life on earth and placed flowers right at the center of things, along with us humans. I agree with him completely: we belong together.

*   *   *

Once upon a time, every single flower in the world was a wildflower. Wildflowers are as much the heart-beat of our planet as the oceans. All living creatures interact with wildflowers whether they know it or not. For 130 million years, wildflowers have blessed the earth with their amazing skill sets and stunning beauty – absolutely free of charge! But what do we really know about them beyond those Sunday drives into the country where we marvel at their colors and variety and maybe stop to pick a bouquet to take home?

Wildflowers are, without exaggeration, the unsung heroes of the planet; they are a powerful force that truly sustains a complex web of interdependent creatures. Without wildflowers our planet would not only be a sadder place, but life as we know it would not exist. You won't ever catch wildflowers bragging about their accomplishments. They go about their business quietly, unnoticed and largely unobserved. But what work they do! Later in the chapter you'll have the opportunity to inspect Ms. Wildflower's planetary report card and you'll see for yourself what an overachiever she is. I think of wildflowers as feminine beings, participating in the most nurturing, life-sustaining aspects of creation.

A First Look

Let me give you a glimpse of what I know about wildflowers. For a sense of their extraordinary reach and service, here are a few of the things they are doing for us and have been doing for eons:

- Attracting and sustaining beneficial wildlife (the pollinators and others creatures essential to keeping the plant and animal kingdom – and us – going)
- Creating extensive recycling, composting, land repurposing and self-regulating water filtration systems
- Mastering extreme weather survival
- Developing a continent-wide erosion control program
- Nurturing the expansion of a wide range of living organisms
- Doing all of this practical work while giving us the great gift of their beauty

A few other things to know about them: they don't require watering or fertilizing and they filter pollutants and regulate the air quality. Their monetary value is incalculable, both for the food production that they enable and for the services they render to the ecology of the planet.

The State of the Wildflower Today

While humans have been pursuing their human activities, the environment has been in a steady state of decline. For a long time we saw this decline as a necessary tradeoff for the progress of civilization… if we were aware of the decline at all. Now, of course, our culture appears to be locked in a debate over what to blame for the problem – natural climate forces, human activity or some combination of both.

This much I know:

Somewhere around 380 million years ago, plant life covered much of the earth, before the appearance of flower forms. Today, over 90% of the native plants that had flourished here for millions of years are gone, including our wildflowers. This also means that the animal species dependent upon wildflowers for food and shelter have been decimated. Most of us live in cities or suburbs where it's easy to lose awareness of what's happening out in nature, especially since its decline has been happening over a long period of time.

But now we are being forced to notice that essential parts of our entire ecosystem are nearly gone. Suddenly, the changes are happening quickly, right before our eyes. We can't avoid the news that diminishing bee populations may have a dire effect on our food supply; that nearly 1/3 of managed honeybee colonies in the U.S. were lost during the winter of 2012-2013; that monarch butterfly populations, once plentiful in North America, have hit a record low, with reported losses reaching 60% over the 2012-2013 winter; that some of North America's most beloved birds have suffered declines of up to

95% since monitoring began in 1970 (data for the Northern Great Lakes-St. Lawrence region).

Why is this important for us to know? Bees and other pollinators are vital for three-quarters of the world's food crops. No small thing. There are many complex causes for the loss of these essential creatures. Alarms have been raised worldwide, but time is fleeting while the scientific, industrial and governmental debates go on. Habitat continues to be destroyed, heavy pesticides, herbicides and fungicides continue to be used – and all the while death tolls keep rising among the pollinators. No creature – bee, butterfly, bird or human – can fight off the challenge of a parasite or virus if it is stressed by a lack of food and habitat and weakened with sub-lethal doses of chemicals.

Human beings are beginning to realize we have nearly destroyed the lives of the countless creatures needed to grow our food and keep the complex mechanics of our planet chugging along smoothly. As a species, we certainly have a lot to learn when it comes to long-term self-preservation.

What Can We Do?

Grow wildflowers! Because we tend to grow the same few kinds of non-native plants throughout our garden landscapes, we are literally starving the dwindling pollinator populations. Pollinators NEED native plants – a wide array of native plants! In the next chapter I'll explain the symbiotic relationship between wildflowers and pollinators and how it keeps our planet humming, buzzing, tweeting, and chirping along.

But before we pay a visit to the wide, wide world of pollinators, there are some basic definitions I want to give you, relating to wildflowers and other things botanical.

Wildflowers 101

There are several distinctions to be made when we try to determine just what is and what isn't a wildflower.

Are wildflowers and native plants the same thing? A native plant or an indigenous plant is just another name for a wildflower.

What's the difference between a weed and a wildflower? A weed is simply a plant growing somewhere that someone doesn't want it to.

Weeds, aliens and naturalized flowers

Many flowers we think of as wildflowers actually came from somewhere else in the world. They are aliens. Two flowers often thought to be wildflowers are Dandelions and Canada Thistle. Dandelions were

The Canada Thistle and Dandelion are not native to North America but have been here for so long that they are considered to be 'naturalized'.

originally brought over from Europe in the 1600s, although it is not known whether it was intentional or unintentional. Canada Thistle seeds, so the story goes, were brought to North America by Scottish immigrants in order to continue their homeland's tradition of including the beautiful purple thistle blossom into the bridal ceremony. Both of these alien species have made themselves very much at home here. When an alien plant grows prolifically in its new home it is said to have "naturalized." Unfortunately for these two species, they are also, more often than not, considered weeds.

Alien invasions!

Alien plants become "invasive" when they grow aggressively, and spread and displace native vegetation. These plants are generally undesirable because they are difficult and costly to control and can dominate whole habitats, making them environ-

Examples of alien invasions: In North America, gardeners go to great lengths to grow Hydrangeas and Agapanthus. New Zealanders regularly hack Hydrangeas and Agapanthus out of their gardens. In New Zealand they are considered invasive weeds.

mentally destructive in certain situations. Plants that seem to suddenly "take over" are labeled invasive, meaning that they have characteristics in their abilities to disperse and spread that let them do damage to otherwise intact ecological systems. This is a serious problem, both in conservation terms and in economic terms. Removing and managing these invasive plants costs taxpayers over 30 billion dollars a year. Invasive plants take over forest floors and wetlands, wiping out entire eco-systems.

But not all non-native plants are invasive! Just be sure to avoid dangerously invasive plants in your garden plans and, of course, be sure to include a wide selection of wildflowers and native grasses!

You will find several helpful links to identify alien plants in the Resouce Guide.

What's an heirloom plant?

Heirloom plants were brought to North America by people from another part of the world in order to grow familiar food, flowers and other beautiful plants. They are, in effect, non-native. All heirloom plants are open-pollinated plants but not all open-pollinated plants are heirlooms. This is important to understand and will become clearer once you've made it through the next definition. Heirloom plants must be open-pollinated in order to produce seeds that are true to the plant, thereby continuing the plant lineage.

What is open pollination?

Open-pollinated plants grow true from seeds. That means that so long as open-pollination plants are kept away from different plants with which they can cross, they will produce seed that will come "true to type." In other words, the plants in the following generation will resemble the parent plants. No need for human interference in their breeding habits. *Hybrid* plants, on the other hand, require careful management by expert horticulturalists to maintain their desired characteristics.

Open-pollinated plants reproduce themselves in one of two ways: cross-pollination between two plants (via wind, insects or water) or self-pollination (between male and female flower parts contained within the same flower or separate flowers on the same plant).

What is cross-pollination?

I learned about cross-pollination of wildflowers several years ago when I made the mistake of planting two types of penstemon far too close together in the Wildflower Farm gardens. By accident I created my own penstemon hybridizing program!

Here's what happened: for many years we had been growing *Penstemon grandiflorus*.

Ten years ago I was captivated by the dainty beauty of another kind of native penstemon, *Penstemon hirsutus* or Hairy Beardtongue – an ugly name for a soft, pink, rather elegant wildflower!

I thought it might make a great addition to Wildflower Farm's spring and early summer-blooming wildflower offerings. I grew about 50 plants from seed and planted most of them about 50 feet from the pure white Penstemon grandiflorus.

Well, after two years the entire patch of pure white penstemons turned a soft pink; the soft pink

Penstemon digitalis, or Smooth Penstemon, has brilliant white flowers.

The flowers of the Hairy Beardtongue, or Penstemon hirsutus, are a light pink color.

Penstemon hirsutus died off in the shade, and the few I had planted farther away in our rockery and scree garden absolutely took off and thrived! I finally wised up and grew more pure white *Penstemon grandiflorus* from seed and planted them far, far away from the pink *Penstemon hirsutus*. What a great learning experience.

What is a mutant?

All wildflower growers have had the experience of discovering an exceptionally beautiful wildflower created accidentally by nature; a mutant, if you will. For example, an *Echinacea purpurea* that has darker purple pink petals, or one that grows multiple petals all over the seed head. Some of these mutants have become the inspiration for flower breeders. You've no doubt come upon some of these exotic looking mutants in your local garden center – a common place to witness first-hand Echinacea's saturation in the marketplace.

A Most Impressive Report Card

Student: Ms. Wildflower		
Total Years in School: 1.3 million	Total Days Late: 0	Total Days Absent: 0
School Address: North America		

Subject	Grade	Comments
LANGUAGE		
Native Tongue	A+	Ms. Wildflower has shown her skills in building upon the communication of others, enhancing one's thoughts and ability to express what cannot be said in words. She is an excellent listener and not quick to interrupt. Needs to work on speaking up for herself where habitats are concerned.
Communication	B	
MATHEMATICS		
Geometry and Spatial Sense	A+	Ms. Wildflower has fully grasped the concepts of perimeter and area, applying each to real-life situations. She has a deep understanding of important color and shape patterns, knowing the best combinations for pollination and long-term survival.
Patterning and Algebra	A+	
SCIENCE AND TECHNOLOGY		
Biology	A+	Ms. Wildflower has really excelled in the Sciences. Her complete understanding of her important role within the ecosystem has helped her attract the necessary pollinators to sustain herself and others. She has fully grasped the concepts of water and air filtration and has mastered the chemistry behind photosynthesis and carbon sequestration. Finally, I am happy to say that she has almost defied physics, stabilizing soil on slopes in ways no other can.
Chemistry	A+	
Physics	A+	
THE ARTS		
Drama	A+	I can't say enough about Ms. Wildflower's artistic ability. Her talent in dramatic expressions and bold faces is second to none. This semester, she partnered with a classmate, The Wind, to create one of the most beautiful dances I have ever seen, bringing real and imagined music to the ears. In collaboration with her fellow flowers, she continues to paint the land with beautiful colors throughout the season.
Dance	A+	
Music	A+	
Visual Arts	A+	
LEARNING SKILLS/WORK HABITS		
Independence	A+	I have found Ms. Wildflower to be exceptionally independent, never needing to be watered or fertilized. She often takes the initiative in self-sowing, collaborating with the various pollination partners to really put roots down in a calm, non-invasive way. She shares her pollen and nectar when it is available – a greatly appreciated trait, especially in the insect community. Ms. Wildflower has shown determination in survival, continuously adapting to the weather for the best possible outcome.
Initiative	A+	
Team Work	A+	
AREAS OF IMPROVEMENT/AREAS OF STRENGTH		

Ms. Wildflower, you are a wonderfully friendly companion, but I fear that sometimes you are taken advantage of by those who do not have your best interests at heart. Don't be afraid to speak up for yourself to keep from being pushed out of your habitat: you belong here and will be sorely missed should you be eradicated.

You have done a great job completing all assignments over the past 1.3 million years and I have yet to find another student who is as compatible with the pollinator community as you. Continue to persevere through droughts, floods, early and late frosts and heat waves for the benefit of all living organisms. You are truly an inspiration to others and I can't wait to see what you have in store for the next millennium.

Wildflowers Are Wise!

Like the truly wild creatures they are, wildflowers are programmed for survival.

Sometimes wildflowers would rather perish than be manipulated or trapped in any way. Wildflowers can be willful. No matter how cleverly you try to fool them with lights and heat in the greenhouse, they will only wake up from their long winter sleep when they are certain the conditions are right. They are programmed by nature to survive and are tough to trick! Good for you, wildflowers!

Many botanists and agricultural scientists are very familiar with the survival tactics native plants display when human beings attempt to control them. Currently, for example, scientists at the University of Guelph in Ontario, Canada, are trying to find new, hardy native perennials that, unlike most greenhouse-raised plants, require low inputs of fertilizer, water and heat. Essentially, they would be cutting production costs for growers and appealing to the growing number of people interested in integrating native species into their spaces. These researchers have found that some native species simply don't like being started in pots. And, some native plants, I will add, are super easy to grow in pots but then hate remaining in pots for any length of time!

What's a hybrid plant?

A hybrid or cultivated plant is a cross between two different plant varieties to get the valued attributes of each variety. Hybrids are developed for disease resistance, uniformity of size, flowering, color, taste or any other characteristic that might make the plant special. Most plants and seeds for sale in

What is a Genetically Modified or GMO plant?

We are asked all the time at Wildflower Farm if our wildflower and grass seeds are genetically modified, so I felt the need to take the time here to explain the term.

A genetically modified plant is an organism whose genetic characteristics have been altered by scientists using the techniques of genetic engineering. This is a very large and controversial topic. Briefly, genetic modification began in the 1980s when scientists first discovered the ability to transfer specific genes from one plant to another. It started with a tobacco plant with a resistance to antibiotics and moved rapidly to creating cotton that required minimal, if any, pesticide use, as it was engineered to be resistant to insects. Today, GM corn and rice with added nutrient values (particularly vitamins A and C) and a resistance to drought and insect damage are used in third world countries to feed those who might otherwise be starving.

With all that said, none of the species at Wildflower Farm are genetically modified. They don't need to be – they've grown and evolved to tolerate the diversity in insect and animal populations and the varying weather patterns we experience throughout the continent.

Impatiens walleriana have been one of the most popular bedding plants for decades as they offer stunning color that will grow in the shade. Today, you won't find them used in a large portion of North America due to the spread of downy mildew.

North America are hybridized. Hybrid, or hybridized, flowers are easier for the grower to produce and therefore more profitable. Because they are a cross between varieties, the seed produced by hybrids will not grow true to seed. Seedlings grown from a hybrid could exhibit traits of one or both parent plants or turn out to be something totally random and surprising.

Recently hybridized wildflowers or "nativars" have entered the marketplace. In Chapter 2 I'll address the important pollination and food source issues raised by these native cultivars.

Cloning

Cloning is a process whereby the offspring of one plant is genetically identical to the parent from which it came. It is an expensive technique used by growers to fill greenhouses with vast amounts of beautiful flowers, all guaranteed to act exactly as their parents did.

Mass producing plants through cloning creates a monoculture and a whole host of complications. Growing a monoculture crop is a lot like playing Russian roulette: you're toying with the possibility that an entire crop can be decimated by insect or disease.

One of the most popular garden plants in North America, the beloved Impatiens walleriana, has been wiped out by downy mildew in many parts of Eastern, Midwestern and Western U.S., and parts of Ontario, Canada.

More flats of impatiens have been sold than any other annual bedding plant; impatiens ranks fourth in the hanging basket and potted plant category. Plant industry marketers are scrambling to educate garden center sales staff on plant alternatives to offer a whole generation of gardeners hooked on buying millions of dollars' worth of annual Impatiens walleriana plants.

Paying the cost at your local garden center

You've probably noticed that gardening is more expensive these days. Every expense that goes into producing the plants at your local garden center or big box store has gone up. That's because all the overhead expenses have gone up – heating, soil, trays, fancy printed pots and tags. The hidden expenses have gone up as well. Shipping costs are higher than ever and big plant producers must pay royalties for the privilege of growing and selling specific genetic strains of plants. The royalty fees support the very expensive heavy branding campaigns of these large plant producers.

Lots of the heavily advertised, top-selling plants you see at your local garden center are vegetatively propagated or cloned by growers from cuttings. Growing expenses for cuttings are higher than traditionally grown plants, so in order to make a profit, growers must charge garden centers higher prices. At some point in this process the plants are transplanted into larger pots so their perceived value is higher and you, the final customer, feel better about paying more.

Seduced again and again…

Odds are you've been seduced by a plant or two. We all have. Remember that irresistible plant you couldn't take your eyes off? The one who blindsided you with her beauty? There she was, all tarted up, decked out in full bloom, tantalizing you with her full color plant tags, her sassy foliage. You were a goner. You were so carried away you didn't even bother to read the plant tag. You had to have that plant!

Back at home, you finally snap out of your plant lust stupor and read the tag. Curses! Duped again. This plant demands everything your yard isn't. It needs sun and you have shade; it needs rich, loamy soil - not the sandy dirt known as your backyard. What's a plant luster to do?

You probably know what I'm going to say. If you were growing wildflowers, you would have a lot less to worry about. Once established, native plants don't need fertilizers, herbicides, pesticides, or watering. And many are perennials – year after year they just keep on blooming. Not only is wildflower gardening good for the environment, it saves time and money. And native plants naturally attract diverse varieties of birds, butterflies and good bugs to your property.

If you are looking for a cost effective and aesthetically pleasing way to landscape, incorporating native plants into your outdoor space will reap big benefits. I'm not crusading for total wildflower purity, but I do know that once you start with natives you're going to want more and more of them in your garden. With so many great benefits, what's not to love? 🌼

TWO

Up Close and Personal
with Pollinators

Let me tell you 'bout the birds and the bees and the wildflower seeds...

When I fell in love with native plants I learned how very intertwined are the lives of pollinators and wildflowers – how dependent pollinators are upon wildflowers, wildflowers upon pollinators, and humans upon all of these players for their very existence.

*   *   *

Living the Mad Max Existence

Imagine thriving in a world where unfamiliar, indigestible food is your only option; where the only shelter available to you is meager, inadequate or non-existent, and where each day more and more of your family and friends are disappearing or dying.

Welcome to the day-to-day reality of many pollinators who are struggling to withstand the extreme loss of habitat, are dying of starvation and facing the constant onslaught of poisonous pesticides, herbicides and fungicides. Before we look more deeply into the extraordinary relationship between pollinators and native plants, let's zero in on the amazing process of pollination.

The Deal

Basically the deal between flowers and pretty much the entire living web is this:

- Flowers lure in pollinators with magnificent colors, shapes and scents.

- Pollinators pick up pollen from one flower and transport it to other flowers.
- Reproduction occurs and flower species flourish.
- In return, flowers provide pollinators with nectar, fruits and seeds so they too can survive and enable their species to continue.

Did you know that at least 90% of plants on earth rely on animal pollinators in order to reproduce? Without them, many of the foods we love would disappear. Imagine living without almonds, apples, apricots, coffee and chocolate? Or blueberries, cucumbers, cantaloupes and carrots? It's a dreary thought but let's take a look at what got us to this point.

A (Very Simple) History of Plant Evolution

There's no spoonful of sugar that can make this go down any easier. I will, however, keep it as simple as possible for our present purposes. Whole libraries of textbooks are available should you wish to delve further.

The Earth is approximately 4.54 billion years old. At that time, it was a pretty bleak place. Then, approximately 3.5 billion years ago, *cyanobacteria* changed everything. Taking in intense amounts of carbon dioxide and spitting out oxygen in return, cyanobacteria was the first life form to use the process of photosynthesis. This living, green algae is the reason we are here today.

For a long time, not much changed. The algae kept exchanging carbon dioxide for oxygen and the planet slowly formed an ozone layer. About 542 million years ago, *non-vascular land plants* emerged (non-vascular meaning that they contain no phloem or xylem, the structures used to transport water and nutrients). Four hundred million years ago, the *vascular plants* showed up. With the ability to transport water and nutrients, these plants were considerably larger. (Forgive me for rushing through the eons, but we're only partway through our story.)

One hundred million years later came the *gymnosperms*, the seed-producing plants that relied on the wind for reproduction. This broad category was not greatly diverse, including only conifers, cycads, seed ferns, and ginkgoes. Today, conifers are by far the largest group of gymnosperms.

This brings us to the *angiosperms:* the flowering plants. The ones we've been waiting for. Only developing approximately 130 million years ago, they are relative newcomers to the plant scene.

Angiosperm structure is extensively more complex, and in many ways these plants have perfected the act of reproduction. Just look at how they do it:

- They produce nectar to draw in the pollinators.
- They make pollen that sticks easily to the visitors.
- They create sweet and inviting fruits to protect precious seeds, thus attracting larger animals. The seeds are designed to easily pass through the digestive systems of the animals who eat them…and back into the earth.

These three sources of concentrated super foods – nectar, pollen and fruit – became available through the existence of flowering plants and their highly evolved reproductive systems.

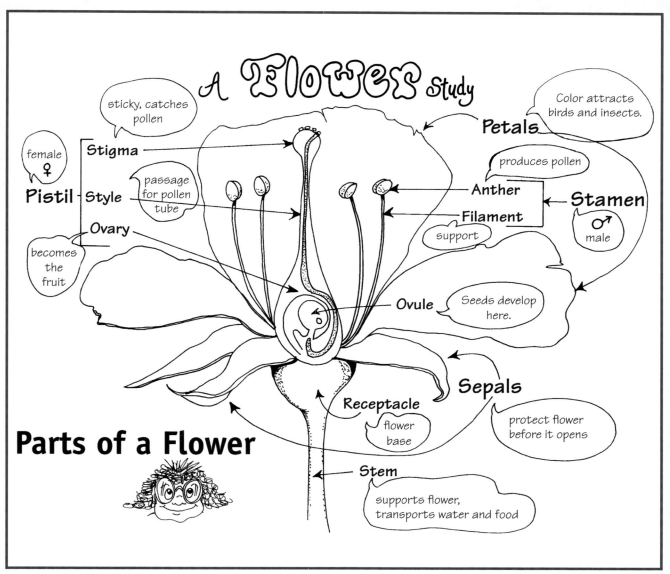

The complexity of the angiosperm developed over millions of years and today we are graced with thousands of variations in color, shape, and texture.

Pollination: a genius idea

Like many great inventions, pollination began with a beta model: wind pollination. As time went on, more clever and efficient means of reproduction began to take shape. Let's start with the earliest.

The Beta Model - Wind Pollination

When the gymnosperms came into existence some 300 million years ago, the only plants that required pollinating were seed ferns, cycads, ginkgoes and conifers. These first plants used the wind to pollinate, a rather inefficient way that has achieved only moderate success as a pollination system.

Even though 90% of plants on earth produce flowers, many important crop plants don't and are wind-pollinated, among them wheat, rice, corn, rye, barley, and oats. Many economically important trees are also wind-pollinated – the pines, spruces, firs and a number of hardwood trees, including several species cultivated for nut production. Wind-pollinated plants do not need showy flowers, nectar or scent. Instead, they produce larger quantities of light, dry pollen from small, plain flowers that can be carried on the wind. Female structures on wind-pollinated plants are adapted to capture the passing pollen from the air; but, with the wind-pollinated system, a majority of the pollen goes to waste, causing allergies and decorating dark cars in a dusty yellow coat.

The Alpha Model – Animal Pollination

Angiosperms (the flowering plants, remember?) create seeds that are fully equipped plant embryos packed in a little enclosed box stuffed full of nutritious food, designed much like a chicken egg. A truly elegant design. Before that can happen, though, a visit from a pollinator is in order. When the pollinator visits a flower to collect nectar and/or pollen, it deliberately or accidentally picks up pollen on its body. As it goes on to forage at other flowers, an effective pollinator will unintentionally drop some of that pollen to a receptive female flower of the same plant species. The end result is a seed filled with all the genetic information, food and protection needed to grow another wildflower.

For animal pollination to be successful, several things must occur:

- The pollinator must touch the female stigma with the same part of its body that contacted the male anther of the first flower.

All grasses, including this Canada Wild Rye, are excellent examples of wind pollination.

- It must deliver enough pollen to fertilize the ovules in the flower.
- It must visit the same plant species regularly enough to deliver the pollen before it is lost.
- If any of these tasks fail, pollination will not take place.

Hi-Tech Seed Transportation Systems

Successful pollination results in the production of seeds. As seeds diversified with the evolution of flowers, their methods of transportation also diversified. It's easy to tell which method a plant uses to spread its seed just by looking at their individual designs.

The birds, butterflies, bats and bugs have been cutting deals with wildflowers for centuries. And one more creature that signed this multi-millennial deal: *Homo sapiens.* Yes, us…

Human Pollinators

The smell, the nectar and the design of flower blossoms are calculated to appeal to pollinators, including human ones. "Humans?" you'll ask. "We have little need for pollen or nectar." Hear me out.

Perhaps for survival's sake, early humans observed the connection between flowers and the subsequent abundance of food. Flowers signal springtime, the coming of warm weather, fertile soil and soon, plenty to eat. When pollination is successful and flowers have made way for fruit, we eat the food and

Method 1 – Simply drop it on the ground and it grows.

Method 2 – Transport that seed via feather-down attachments - as in dandelion or milkweed seed that allow the seed to float upwards and ride for miles.

Method 3 – Attach the seeds with Velcro-like hooks that cling to furry mammal.

Method 4 – Cleverly disguise seed in juicy, colorful berries, devoured by birds – or fruits, devoured by larger animals. The seed passes undigested through their intestinal tracts and is voided and planted miles away.

disperse the seeds, ensuring the continued existence of that species. "Quite a clever plan!" you'll shout.

We humans are hard-wired to love flowers and, it appears, to express our innermost feelings through flowers. Bees and humans both have brains that are based on the same basic building blocks: neurons or nerve cells. These nerve cells are linked together in networks designed to respond to visual stimulation. To enhance their survival, plants developed a successful method to gain the attention of pollinators – all sorts of pollinators. The visual neural pathways in bees and humans are designed to be incapable of being overloaded with floral stimulus. **This means that it is impossible to fill the brain of a human being or a bee with images of too many flowers!**

The Emotional Side of the Human-Wildflower Connection

Through time, the human race has integrated flowers into powerful rituals and rites of passage, such as birth, courtship and bereavement. We know now that flowers trigger remembrance with their fragrance and color. They touch our hearts in ways difficult to understand. We have a powerful neurological link with them, it appears. Let me tell you a story that illustrates my point.

A Friendship Through Wildflowers

Dana and I bumped into one another on Facebook one late December morning, not long ago. I needed a blast of color to course through my soul so I posted one of my favorite images of the purple spiked blazingstar. Suddenly, there was Dana typing madly onto my Facebook page…

"I have an in-progress tattoo that is full of my favorite prairie flowers, and the blazingstar is one of them. It really brightened my day to see your beautiful photo!"

I asked her to tell me more about her tattoo – it sounded so amazing! She replied that it was going to include Cardinal Flower, ironweed (her favorite), blazingstar, goldenrod and different-colored coneflowers.

That was the start of our wildflower friendship. I soon learned the reason behind her tattoo: it was to be a memorial to her mother.

"My connection to wildflowers came from my mother, who fostered in me a love of the Earth and the natural world," Dana wrote. "She was a self-taught gardener and naturalist. Growing up, our bookshelves were loaded with wildlife and wildflower field guides. My mother homeschooled us so we spent lots of time creek-walking, hiking and exploring Cleveland's extensive park system. My mom battled cancer for almost a decade. Before she died she chose to be buried completely naturally at Ohio's only green burial site, Foxfield Preserve. She is buried in an Ohio prairie ecosystem and has completed the cycle of life and returned to the Earth. The wildflowers keep her with me always.:) I plan on adding to it annually in memory of my mom."

Dana's wildflower tattoo is a beautiful tribute to her mother and a wonderful reminder of the connection all humans have with the wild. Dana's tattoo includes Cardinal Flower, Canada Wild Rye, Joe-Pye Weed, Big Bluestem and Blazingstar.

If ever I needed further confirmation of the deeply-rooted emotional connection between humans and flowers, I had it with Dana's story.

* * *

Non-Human Pollinators

Non-human pollinators have co-evolved with wildflowers for millennia. Huge challenges have arisen that threaten the very existence of many pollinators: habitats are being wiped out, pesticide and fungicide use continues, and the hybrid and non-native plants that are so abundant in today's ecosystems cannot provide the various pollinators with adequate nutrition or shelter.

There are four main categories of insect pollinators: bees and wasps, beetles, moths and butterflies, and flies. On top of that are the non-insect pollinators: birds, bats, and a few other vertebrates. Without getting too scientific, let me introduce you to the team.

Bees

Probably the most familiar of the pollinator family, bees are also considered the most efficient as many have developed one of two highly specialized structures – the scopa or the corbicula. The former meaning a patch of stiff hairs located on

Bees, no matter their size, are extremely efficient pollinators due to their specialized structures.

the hind legs or underside of the abdomen to gather and carry pollen; the latter meaning a patch of hairs curved inward creating a basket-like structure on the hind legs that effectively acts the same way as a scopa.

Bees also have specially developed eyes capable of picking up ultraviolet (UV) wavelengths: a shorter wavelength than the one you and I use to perceive the world around us. When a human looks at a flower, they see any number of colors present in, what we call, the visible light region of the full electromagnetic spectrum. These are the colors of the rainbow. When a bee looks at a flower, it sees much more.

Once considered a tolerable species kept around for honey production, bees are now recognized and celebrated as significant pollinators of commercial vegetables, native and non-native flowers, and certain flowering trees and shrubs.

In North America, we have a number of native bee species – close to 4,000 – often categorized into 6 main families. And while there is a plethora of information I could pass along to you, I'll keep it fairly short and simple.

1. **Andrenidae** (mining bees) – solitary bees, dwelling underground in individual burrows.

2. **Apidae** (bumble, carpenter, honey, and a few others) – hive-dwelling bees living in fairly large colonies. A great variation in appearance exists within this family as both the very hairy black and yellow native bumblebee and fairly non-hairy, golden-colored non-native European honey bee are a part.

3. **Colletidae** (plaster bees) – solitary and ground-dwelling. Commonly known as the plaster bee, the females create sealed, water-proof broods to protect ground-laid eggs from fungal attacks.

4. **Halictidae** (sweat bees) - distinguished by their small size and shiny, green and blue metallic colors, these bees live from one extreme to the other: some are completely solitary while others are communal. There are also those that are semi-social, gathering only for egg-laying and others that are eusocial: gathering to share the load in caring for young. These bees dwell underground and are often the ones you see flying around you on a hot summer day.

5. **Megachilidae** (leafcutter and mason bees) – solitary bees that live in tubular nests in soil. Crafty creatures, the Megachilidae bees use holes abandoned by other insects. Nests are forged with leaf cuttings or mud, depending on the species.

6. **Melittidae** (oil-collecting bees) – an uncommon bee family, these bees are solitary and ground-dwelling. Commonly known as oil-collecting bees, they collect oil from various flowers to fashion parts of their living quarters.

The majority of our native bees in North America are solitary and ground-dwelling. In fact, the communal Apidae family of bees comprises only about 2% of the total, leaving 98% to lead solitary or semi-solitary lives.

North America has also seen the introduction of the European honey bee: a prolific pollinator in the agricultural business responsible for a good part of North American crop pollination. In recent years, there has been a significant increase in the discussion surrounding honey bee declines – a discussion worthy of our time and effort, as so much of our food production is dependent on their success.

The reasons behind the disappearance of European honey bees are constantly changing. The information presented in this book is as up-to-date as possible and if this is a topic that you are even remotely interested in, I encourage you to delve into the research a little further yourself.

A Bee-Decline Timeline

Despite slowly declining bee numbers before 1997, panic among farmers and environmentalists set in only after 2005, when record declines were announced. In 2007, apiaries began to report 30-70% losses in their hives. With

no real understanding of the causes behind these declines, the term "colony collapse disorder" was established. Over the next several years, millions of dollars were put into research, with the main suspect always being pesticides, which is where neonicotinoids come into play. This previously common household pesticide was banned in the U.K. in 2009. In 2012, a new hypothesis was brought to the table: mites and viruses. It was thought that pesticides weakened the bees and made them vulnerable to the viruses carried by mites. Of course, all along the way there has been much protest by environmental groups to ban neonicotinoids worldwide. As of this book's publication, this has not yet come to fruition.

Today, the suggestion is that while pesticides have obvious negative effects, fungicides are playing just as strong a role in the declination of bee populations across North America. Much like the pesticide-virus interaction, it has been suggested that certain fungicides weaken the immune system subjecting bees to the effects of Nosema infection, a parasitic fungus often found in beehives. More funding and research will continue to be put into this challenging endeavour in hopes of coming to any sort of conclusion.

It is important to note that native bees do a much better job when it comes to pollinating the species that exist here. European honey bees are finicky – they don't like flying when it's too cold, too hot or too wet. The window of pollination opportunity has, then, shrunk quite drastically. But native bees don't mind these temperature fluctuations and many species can withstand a light rain. Still in doubt? One source has stated that an apple orchard normally pollinated by 40,000 honey bees could be pollinated just as effectively by 250 native blue orchard mason bees. Impressive.

Wasps

A highly feared collection of insects, wasps are not the most efficient pollinators by a long shot. The majority of wasps are simply not designed for the task: smooth, hairless bodies and short tongues make the act of gathering pollen and nectar almost impossible. Instead, they choose flowers with flat heads or even easier sources of sugar, such as rotting fruit. Some wasps, however, do provide pollination and this should not be overlooked. Meet the pollen

Wasps aren't great pollinators but they still take advantage of the sugary nectar found in so many wildflowers, like this Rattlesnake Master.

wasp. A small family of about 12 species, pollen wasps sustain themselves and their young by actively gathering pollen and nectar.

Beetles

Of the approximate 350,000 known beetle species across the globe, about 30,000 of them reside in and are native to North America. Beetles are believed to be the first insect pollinators, first taking on the challenge some 130 million years ago. The flowers that existed at the time were much different than the flowers of today. Evolution has changed flower structures, methods of reproduction and means of attracting pollinators, but beetles have stayed relatively the same. That is to say, the evolution of beetles has not kept up with the evolution of flowers. The diversity and sheer number of beetles, however, compensates for that lack of evolution; many flowers worldwide and across North America are, even today, heavily pollinated by various beetles of the Coleoptra family.

Moths

Moths, a part of the Lepidoptera family, are an important pollinator for many night-blooming species despite their crop-destroying larvae. With more than 10,000 species living across North America, moths provide an essential form of passive pollination; that is, they do not gather pollen, but simply pick it up accidentally as they are sipping nectar. Some flowers require moth pollination and release very specific scents at night to attract the appropriate moth. Several yucca species and the

The goldenrod soldier beetle is a common garden friend that helps to pollinate and whose larvae munch on aphids and small caterpillars.

Common Evening Primrose (both North American natives) are guilty of such trickery.

Butterflies

The more appreciated relative of the Lepidoptera family, butterflies, are seen far more often than moths, but in reality are much less prevalent – with

Butterflies, like this pearly crescentspot resting on some 'Silver King' Artemisia, are regular visitors to flower gardens where they will sip nectar and gather small pollen grains with their furry bodies.

12.5 moth species for every 1 butterfly species in North America. Butterflies are not the greatest pollinators. Their long, straw-like mouthparts (called a proboscis) make it easy for them to reach the nectar within the flower without getting close to the pollen-producing anthers. But because their bodies have short hairs, they can accidentally pick up and transfer small pollen grains between flowers.

The Monarch-Milkweed Relationship. A good majority of you will have heard that monarchs need milkweed to survive. It's true. Milkweed (Asclepias) is the only plant monarch caterpillars will use for food and the only plant on which monarch adults will lay their eggs.

The monarch life cycle begins with an egg laid on the bottom of a milkweed leaf. The egg hatches, producing a small larva or caterpillar. This caterpillar sustains itself with the plant on which it hatched and moves on when that plant becomes bare. The caterpillar continues to eat and grow for about 17 days until it is time to pupate. Inside the chrysalis, or cocoon, the pupa takes about eight days to develop into an adult – a process called metamorphism. Once emerged from the chrysalis, the adult monarch butterfly will no longer feed on the milkweed plant, but on nectar from various flower sources. After mating, the monarch begins the cycle once more. The last generation for the year is triggered as a migratory generation: they do not grow reproductive organs and instead use that energy to travel south from northern states and provinces to California or Mexico where they refuel and mate. Adults that have mated will begin their journey back north begin-

As an adult, the monarch no longer requires only milkweed to survive and you will find them feasting on nectar from a variety of flowers like the Purple Blazingstar pictured here.

ning in March. Along the way, they lay their eggs on milkweed, the adults usually dying afterwards. The first generation of the year begins with eggs that were laid between somewhere between Mexico and Canada. Three to four generations will take place, each moving successively more north before the cold weather triggers another southward migration.

The Problem. Monarch numbers have been in decline for a number of years and much like the honey bee population decline, there doesn't seem to be one answer. However, one issue is prevalent among those studying the subject: pesticides and herbicides.

Pesticides are an obvious problem: they are sprayed to kill the insects that are often the cause of damage to field crops. Herbicides, however, may not be so obvious. The function of an herbicide is the chemical removal of weeds – those who compete for water, nutrients and light. And therein lies the problem: milkweed is considered a competitor…a weed. The milkweed plant also contains a cardiac glycoside, a poisonous chemical known to be fatal for agricultural livestock. The systematic removal of milkweed from agricultural fields results in fewer potential egg-laying and food sources than are necessary to facilitate a smooth migration.

Flies

One might not think of flies as pollinators, but one may also not realize that the realm of flies exists far beyond that pesky housefly. The bee fly family is so named for its resemblance to bumblebees. It's not so much their color patterns that brought on the name, but the way they maneuver around flowers. Bee flies have long, straw-like mouthparts that allow them, like butterflies and bumblebees, to reach the nectar within the flower. In the process, their long, bristly hairs rustle up the pollen that becomes attached to the fly, allowing pollen to be transported. And before we go dismissing houseflies as simply a nuisance, remember that the carrot seeds you planted are the result of housefly pollination.

Note: The insects pictured in this chapter have been identified to the best of my knowledge. With

This hoverfly, *Toxomeric marginatus,* is another type of fly pollinator whose adult and larval phases are extremely beneficial.

that said, I'd like to point out that I'm not an entomologist and so mistakes are inevitable.

Birds

Ornithophily, or pollination by birds, is not the most popular method of pollination in North America. While much more diverse in the tropics, we do have one very notable example in North America. The hummingbird. This easily recognizable bird is the world's smallest and has adapted quite well to the incredible diversity of flowering plants. They see in the ultraviolet light spectrum, as do bees, and their tongues are shaped perfectly to feed on nectar from tubular-shaped flowers. Plants that are designed for hummingbird pollination are specifically engineered for this task: they are often bright red, orange, and yellow, unscented, produce large quantities of pollen – and as previously mentioned, are tubular-shaped.

As a hummingbird seeks nectar (which, on average, it must do every 10 minutes), its long beak gathers pollen grains. Moving quickly between flowers allows cross-pollination to occur fairly easily.

Bats

Bats are not a source for pollination in North America. However, throughout the tropics and in desert climates, bats are extremely important to the production of bananas, avocadoes and cashews among many others. Within North America, though, you'd be hard-pressed to see a bat pollinating any of your plants.

Starving Our Pollinators

The landscapes for our homes, schools, businesses and places of worship consist of 80% lawn and 20% plants. Over 80% of these plants come from else-where in the world. These alien plants are not the plants that pollinators are genetically programmed to eat, find shelter in or that assist them in successfully reproducing. We are ignoring the utility of wild-flowers in favor of other kinds of plants.

Research seems to indicate that not only do the majority of non-native plants provide sub-standard nutrition to pollinators, but that our stark and overly tidy landscapes are not useful to pollinators. A recent study published in the Proceedings of the National Academy of Sciences found that bumblebees prefer to forage at sites with a greater variety of plants and more floral choices. Bumblebees like landscapes that offer lots of wildflowers and native grasses – a biodiverse meadow!

Though European honey bees were imported to pollinate our crops, our native wild bumblebees and other insects pollinate a significant portion and may be more productive. A crop monoculture or a residential landscape lacking native plants is starving our pollinators. Bumblebees, for example, rely on wildflowers for a steady supply of pollen and nectar. When farming or development destroys forests and meadows, we destroy the home and food source of our key pollinators.

How Wild-Sourced Foods Benefit Human Health

I was excited to learn about the dramatic nutritional difference between the wild plants in the

Wildflowers provide native bees with the essentials for survival.

Are Native Plants and 'Nativars' Nutritionally Superior?

Studies conducted on wild human food versus hybridized versions of the same food are now proving that the native foods have higher nutritional value. It's possible that this affects our pollinators as well, and that non-native, hybridized or genetically modified plants offer pollinators nutritionally inferior food. A number of studies underway are comparing the nutritional values of native and hybrid plants. I was particularly interested in a study happening at the University of Vermont that is looking at the ability of native flowers and 'nativars' (hybridized wildflowers) to not only attract pollinators but support them. More information on the subject can be found in the digital Bibliography and Resource Guide pages of www.tamingwildflowers.com. Anecdotal evidence is that 'nativars' tend to not be as robust as real wildflowers. My own experience is that they tend to be short-lived compared to their wild, non-hybridized cousins. But the jury is still out.

My concern is that if wildflowers are over-bred, pollinators will suffer. When many beautiful heirloom flowers are over-bred they lose their scent and often the pollen they produce becomes sterile, with decreased nutritional value for the precious pollinators.

original human diet and the man-made varieties we eat today. For example, wild tomatoes have up to thirty times more cancer-fighting lycopene than most supermarket tomatoes. The wild purslane has six more times vitamin E than spinach and fourteen times more omega-3 fatty acids. And purslane has seven times more beta-carotene than carrots.

Wild fruits and vegetables are the original low-glycemic foods. Most edible wild foods are higher in protein and fiber and lower in sugars than their heirloom equivalents we find at the grocery store. Health experts urge us to eat a diet high in fiber and low in sugar and rapidly digested carbohydrates. This so-called low-glycemic diet has been linked to a reduced risk for obesity, diabetes, cancer and heart disease.

Wildflowers Benefit Pollinator Health

I'm betting that researchers will find that wildflowers produce the highest quality nutrition for the pollinators that sustain their species. And when we have highly nutritional food plants, the animals at the top of the food chain – ourselves – are winners, as well.

Now What?

For me, it's simple: no matter your gardening preferences, wildflowers can and should be part of the picture. They'll grow just about anywhere, from a container on your balcony to your cutting garden; from your flower borders to your vegetable or community garden.

Have a little extra space? Start a pollinator patch. Not sure what species you should start with? Have

Wildflowers, like hardy Echinacea species, are a great source of food for our native bumblebees.

I got some beauties to show you! Let's move on to Chapter 3, where I'll introduce you to 60 of my favorite, easy-to-grow wildflowers. Later on, I'll show you how to grow them from seed, where to grow them and how to make stunning wildflower arrangements. It's time to grace our fair land with the beauty and wisdom of wildflowers, including three native grasses you should know about.. And trust me, it's an exciting time. 🌸

27

THREE

The Wildflowers

I never planned to fall in love with wildflowers. In fact, my interest in wildflowers began purely as a business relationship. I was growing thousands of high maintenance annual and perennial flowers for my pick-your-own flower farm. I needed to grow more flowers but couldn't afford the time or money it would cost to grow more high maintenance flowers. What to do? Over and over, my research led to the same conclusion: perennial wildflowers and native grasses lived longer, needed minimal maintenance, and were stunningly beautiful in both garden and vase. Then and there, this desperate and exhausted gardener began to grow wildflowers from seed. And I haven't looked back.

* * *

I am excited to introduce you to 60 of my favorite wildflowers and native grasses. Some will be familiar friends you have seen or grown in their native or hybridized form and many of these wildflowers will be entirely new to you. It still shocks me that so many of these exquisite and garden-worthy plants are unfamiliar to North Americans. It is my honor to share the beauty and wisdom of these ancient, easy-care plants with you.

Chapter Notes

Bloom Times

In each plant profile you'll see that instead of indicating the specific months a wildflower blooms, I have given the phase of the season. This is because, while a flower may bloom in different months in each state, flowers across the country will always bloom in the same phase of a season, regardless of the region they're planted in. For example, Tennessee Coneflower will bloom in a different month in the warmer climate of Arkansas than it will in the colder region of New England. However, Tennessee Coneflowers in any region will always bloom sometime in early summer through early fall.

The species listed here are organized into four overarching bloom-phase categories: Spring; Late Spring-Early Summer; Summer; and Fall. Within these categories, I have grouped certain plant families. Most of the flowers within these families will bloom in their designated blooming category – but always refer to the "bloom time" given for each, to be sure.

Germination Instructions and Codes

The following codes – NPT, SC, CMS – refer to the native species listed in this chapter.

- **No Pre-treatment Necessary (NPT)** – The seed needs only cold, dry storage before planting. It will germinate upon sowing in a warm location. The seed needs light to germinate, so do not cover after sowing. Water the seeds from the bottom as necessary by sitting the container in a

saucer of water. Do not let the soil dry out until the seedlings are established.

- **Seed Needs Scarification (SC)** – Rub the seed between two sheets of sandpaper to scrape the seed coat. Stop if seeds are being crushed. Then mix the seed with moist (but not wet) sterile growing medium. Place the mixture in a labeled, sealed plastic bag and store it in the refrigerator for six to eight weeks. Note: Some seed may germinate in the storage bag if it is moist stratified too long. If sprouting occurs, plant immediately. Another method is to sow seed outdoors in late autumn so that they may overwinter.

- **Cold, Moist Stratification (CMS)** – Mix the seed with moist (not wet) sterile growing medium. Place the mixture in a labeled, sealed plastic bag and store it in the refrigerator for six to eight weeks. (Note: Some seed may germinate in the storage bag if moist stratified too long. If sprouting occurs, plant immediately.) Another method is to sow seed outdoors in late autumn so that they may overwinter.

For further instruction on cold, moist stratifying techniques and germinating seeds, see Chapter 5.

Spring Beauties

Just the very thought of spring-blooming wildflowers makes me happy. Their shapes, soft colors and the wonder of their much-anticipated appearance thrill me each spring. And I'm not alone… ask any gardener, and they'll likely jump at the chance to tell you all about their favorite spring wildflowers; how cunning, petite and adorable they are and how they are bowled over by each flower's exquisite beauty.

Many spring-blooming wildflowers are ephemeral, meaning after they wake up in the spring – foliage, flowers and all – they quietly return to sleep again, leaving plenty of room for the larger, later-blooming flowers.

Spring-blooming wildflowers have another characteristic in common: they are flowering earlier and earlier! Scientists are finding that plants keep shifting their flowering times as the climate continues to warm.

Many of the well-known spring wildflowers are tricky to grow from seed. Luckily, many of these early beauties are easy to find in plant form – either as pure native plants or as nativars.

Golden Alexanders *Zizia aurea*

This spring-blooming beauty looks like a combination of Golden Yarrow and Queen Anne's Lace. Golden Alexanders, a member of the carrot family, blooms beautifully alongside late-blooming tulips, Shooting Stars, Wild Lupines, and columbine and adds vibrancy to early season fresh flower arrangements. The blooms will last three to five days. As an added bonus, Golden Alexanders forms dark purple seed heads that look earthy and elegant in summer and fall arrangements.

GOLDEN ALEXANDERS

Height: 1' - 2'
Color: Yellow
Bloom Time: Mid-spring through early summer
Light: Full sun to part shade
Soil: Sand, loam, clay
Moisture: Medium to moist
Germination: CMS
Grows well in containers at least 12" deep
Not Everlasting
Not Deer Resistant
Salt Tolerant
Not Edible
Pollination Partners: Look for short-tongued bees, wasps, flies, and beetles on the Golden Alexanders who are there for both the pollen and the nectar. Even though many pollinators visit, Golden Alexanders self-pollinate. Caterpillars of the black swallowtail and Ozark swallowtail feed on the leaves and flowers.
Native to:
USA (AL, AR, CT, DC, DE, FL, GA, IA, IL, IN, KS, KY, LA, MA, MD, ME, MI, MN, MO, MS, MT, NC, ND, NE, NH, NJ, NY, OH, OK, PA, RI, SC, SD, TN, TX, VA, VT, WI, WV)
CAN (MB, NB, NS, ON, QC)

Pasque Flower · *Anemone patens*

Pasque Flowers do everything right. In spring, they burst into bloom exactly when I can't stand another minute of floral deprivation! Their cunningly shaped purple, pink or white velvety flowers make me swoon. Then, as if that weren't enough, Pasque Flowers' puffy seed heads maintain their exquisite round form for many weeks and make magical, airy miniature bouquets.

PASQUE FLOWER

Height: <1'
Color: Purple
Bloom Time: Mid through late spring
Light: Full sun to part shade
Soil: Sand to loam
Moisture: Dry to medium
Germination: CMS
Grows well in containers at least 10" deep
Not Everlasting
Deer Resistant
Not Salt Tolerant
Not Edible
Pollination Partners: Sweat bees are attracted to the Pasque Flower, which offers abundant pollen and tiny amounts of nectar. The foliage contains a blistering agent and is poisonous, a feature that successfully discourages animals (and humans) from munching on these beauties. Be cautions, as the chemical compound within this flower is strong enough to damage skin.
Native to:
USA (AK, CO, IA, ID, IL, KS, MI, MN, MT, ND, NE, NM, SD, TX, UT, WA, WI, WY)
CAN (AB, BC, MB, NT, ON, SK, YT)

Prairie Smoke ❧ *Geum triflorum*

It's love at first sight when you behold the silky, flowing plumes of Prairie Smoke. As the small, reddish pink blossoms go to seed, they open to create a dazzling effect that resembles smoke hovering close to the ground. They are one of the first flowers to bloom in spring in our scree garden. Prairie Smoke flowers and seed heads are on very short stems, so they work beautifully in small displays. Find a tiny vase and incorporate them into miniature spring blooming arrangements.

PRAIRIE SMOKE
Height: <1'
Color: Red
Bloom Time: Early through late spring
Light: Full sun to part shade
Soil: Sand to loam
Moisture: Dry
Germination: CMS
Grows well in containers at least 10" deep
Not Everlasting
Not Deer Resistant
Not Salt Tolerant
Not Edible
Pollination Partners: Bumblebees seeking nectar will force their way into the flower, which is closed so strongly that very few pollinators have enough strength to push through.
Native to:
USA (AZ, CA, CO, IA, ID, IL, MI, MN, MT, ND, NM, NV, NY, OR, SD, UT, WA, WI, WY)
CAN (AB, BC, MB, NT, ON, SK, YT)

Shooting Star ❧ *Dodecatheon meadia*

This is one of the more unusual wildflowers! So named for its shooting star-like appearance, this flower has a fiery yellow center that points downward and bright purple, pink, or white petals that taper away from the ground. Shooting Star is an ancient ancestor of the Cyclamen houseplant. The blooming period for this unusual plant lasts about a month during late spring. As spring fades, so too does the Shooting Star, pushing roots for next year's growth. The pink Dark Throated Shooting Star or *Dodecatheon pulchellum* is also quite lovely. A short-lived but glorious cut flower, Shooting Star looks stunning in lush spring arrangements.

SHOOTING STAR

Height: 1' - 2'
Color: White
Bloom Time: Mid through late spring
Light: Full sun to part shade
Soil: Sand, loam
Moisture: Medium
Germination: CMS
Grows well in containers at least 10" deep
Not Everlasting
Deer Resistant
Not Salt Tolerant
Not Edible
Pollination Partners: Queen bumblebees frequent the Shooting Star using a method of pollination called "buzz pollination," whereby pollen is released from the anthers through rapid vibrations of the bee's muscles. The tiny seeds are too small to be of much interest to birds.
Native to:
  USA (AL, AR, DC, FL, GA, IA, IL, IN, KS, KY, LA, MD, MI, MN, MO, MS, NC, NY, OH, OK, PA, SC, TN, TX, VA, WI, WV)
  CAN (MB)

Smooth Solomon's Seal ❧ *Polygonatum biflorum*

All season long, the arching stems of Smooth Solomon's Seal seem to dance through my shade gardens. This member of the Lily family does not grow upwards, but arcs almost horizontally across the garden as if it were top-heavy. It blooms in the spring, with cream-colored, capsule-shaped blossoms dangling from the stems. Solomon's Seal's oval-shaped leaves alternate in almost a zigzag pattern up each stem to create a sort of spiral effect. The flowers are stunning in spring and early summer arrangements, and the foliage is a true workhorse in bouquets and arrangements all summer long.

SMOOTH SOLOMON'S SEAL

Height: Height: 1' - 2'
Color: White
Bloom Time: Mid through late spring
Light: Full sun to full shade
Soil: Sand, loam
Moisture: Medium to moist
Germination: Very difficult; luckily, Smooth Solomon's Seal is very easy to find at any garden center or from a friend's garden.
Dramatic by itself in containers at least 15" deep
Not Everlasting
Not Deer Resistant
Not Salt Tolerant
Not Edible
Pollination Partners: Attracts long-tongued bees, including bumblebees, digger bees, and carpenter bees. The Ruby-Throated Hummingbird also visits; attracts songbirds.
Native to:
USA (AL, AR, CT, DC, DE, FL, GA, IA, IL, IN, KS, KY, LA, MA, MD, ME, MI, MN, MO, MS, MT, NC, ND, NE, NH, NJ, NM, NY, OH, OK, PA, RI, SC, SD, TN, TX, VA, VT, WI, WV, WY)
CAN (MB, ON, QC, SK)

Wild Columbine/Eastern Columbine *Aquilegia canadensis*

One of the most familiar, most beautiful, and most beloved of wildflowers, Wild Columbine has cunningly designed, hollow, spur-like flowers that appear to be two flowers in one - an inner yellow flower surrounded by an elegantly spurred, red outer flower. As an added benefit, hummingbirds and songbirds find columbine irresistible! Blooming in late spring, it reaches a height of one to three feet. It does best in dappled shade, but grows easily in full sun, too. Wild Columbine flowers look beautiful in bouquets and will last three to five glorious days.

WILD/EASTERN COLUMBINE

Height: Height: 1' - 3'
Color: Red and yellow
Bloom Time: Mid-spring through early summer
Light: Full sun, part shade, full shade
Soil: Sand, loam, clay
Moisture: Dry to medium
Germination: CMS
Grows well in containers at least 12" deep
Everlasting: Seed pods
Deer Resistant
Salt Tolerant
Not Edible
Pollination Partners: Honey bees, native bees, butterflies, moths, bumblebees and the Ruby-Throated Hummingbird visit the flowers for nectar. Because Wild Columbine's foliage is toxic, it is pretty much ignored by animals. Finches and other seed-eating birds will eat the seeds.
Native to:
USA (AL, AR, CT, DC, DE, FL, GA, IA, IL, IN, KS, KY, MA, MD, ME, MI, MN, MO, MS, NC, ND, NE, NH, NJ, NY, OH, OK, PA, RI, SC, SD, TN, TX, VA, VT, WI, WV)
CAN (MB, NB, ON, QC, SK)

Late Spring – Early Summer

Early summer can be rather bereft of beauty in the traditional garden – the tulips are long gone and summer blooms haven't kicked in yet. In contrast, the wildflower garden is a riot of color as spring transitions into early summer! The late spring wildflower garden is a very busy place indeed. I enjoy working side-by-side with the droves of hard-working bumblebees.

Even on the coolest days in June, these pollinators are out and about. The queen begins in early spring, and later in June, the workers methodically pollinate every single blue, yellow and white Baptisia, Beardtongue, Harebell, Spiderwort and Coreopsis blossom. Honey bees, though, are the prima donnas of the pollinator world and will only work in ideal conditions: warm weather and no rain.

Splendid bouquet-making opportunities await you in the endlessly entertaining world that is early summer in the wildflower garden!

Beardtongue ❧ *Penstemon grandiflorus*

The softly glowing pink spikes and distinctive blooms of Beardtongue are a welcome sight in my rockery and scree gardens each spring. If you have a super sandy or gravelly soil, you will want to grow these absolutely gorgeous flowers. The blue-green coloration on their foliage is stunning. I use both the foliage and flowers in late spring arrangements. The flowers will last four to seven days as a cut flower.

BEARDTONGUE

Height: 2' - 4'
Color: Pink
Bloom Time: Late spring into early summer
Light: Full sun to part shade
Soil: Sand
Moisture: Dry to medium
Germination: CMS
Grows well in container 12" or deeper
Not Everlasting
Deer Resistant
Not Salt Tolerant
Not Edible
Pollination Partners: Flowers are cross-pollinated by bumblebees, wasps, sweat bees and other long- and short-tongued bees. Attractive to butterflies and moths, and attracts hummingbirds.
Native to:
  USA (CO, CT, IA, IL, IN, KS, MA, MI, MN, MO, MT, ND, NE, NM, OH, OK, SD, TX, WI, WY)
  CAN (NB, NS, ON, QC)

Blanketflower ❧ *Gaillardia aristata*

One of the best known and beloved wildflowers, Blanketflower is native to open, hot plains. This drought-tolerant and adaptable wildflower boasts beautiful, bright red, daisy-like flowers with bronze-to-yellow colored tips. These stunning flowers can reach up to three inches in diameter. Blanketflower thrives in heat and will provide a non-stop supply of bright and cheerful cut flowers throughout the summer. Deadhead Blanketflower every two weeks, and you will be gifted with an endless supply of cut flowers well into the fall!

BLANKETFLOWER
Height: 1' - 2'
Color: Red and yellow
Bloom Time: Early summer through early fall
Light: Full sun
Soil: Sand to loam
Moisture: Dry to medium
Germination: NPT
Excellent in containers 12" or deeper
Not Everlasting
Not Deer Resistant
Salt Tolerant
Not Edible
Pollination Partners: This plant is frequently visited by native and honey bees, as well as many butterfly species, including the Edwards' fritillary. It is also visited by several moth species, including the cryptic moth. The Dakota skipper is highly linked to Gaillardia, making the flower an indicator species for the health of this particular butterfly. The soft-winged flower beetle is an important pollinator in western North America.
Native to:
 USA (AZ, CA, CO, CT, ID, IL, MA, MI, MN, MT, ND, NH, NM, NY, OR, SD, UT, WA, WI, WY)
 CAN (AB, BC, MB, NT, ON, QC, SK, YT)

Blanket Flower
Gaillardia aristata

Blue Flax, Wild Blue Flax ❦ *Linum lewisii*

Every morning, Wild Blue Flax is covered with an abundance of pastel blue blooms. By late afternoon, these have all fallen off and are replaced the next day by new blooms. Blue Flax stems look very fragile, but are tough and fibrous. They are related to Linum usitatissimum (Cultivated Flax), another flax native from the Middle East that has been grown for its fibers. They have been a key ingredient in linen cloth for thousands of years. Though Blue Flax flowers do not last at all as cut flowers, the seed pods that form in mid-summer look gorgeous in summer and fall bouquets and arrangements.

BLUE FLAX, WILD BLUE FLAX

Height: 1' - 2'
Color: Pastel blue
Bloom Time: Late spring into early summer
Light: Full sun
Soil: Sand, loam
Moisture: Dry to medium
Germination: CMS
Excellent in containers 12" or deeper
Everlasting: Seed Pods
Not Deer Resistant
Not Salt Tolerant
Not Edible
Pollination Partners: The flowers are pollinated by sweat bees, leafcutter bees and some mining bee species that suck nectar. Syrphid, muscoid, and dagger flies tend to feed on the pollen. Wild birds such as pheasants and grouse will eat the seeds.
Native to:
USA (AK, AR, AZ, CA, CO, ID, KS, LA, MI, MN, MT, ND, NE, NM, NV, OK, OR, SD, TX, UT, WA, WV, WY)
CAN (AB, BC, MB, NT, NU, ON, QC, SK, YT)

Harebell ❧ *Campanula rotundifolia*

As delicate looking as Harebell appears to be, this sturdy wildflower blooms for well over six weeks and lasts from six to ten days as a cut flower. A short wildflower, growing only about a foot in height, Campanula's delicate, bell-shaped, blue-purple flowers will delight you. Growing these, you will experience many months of blooming, right from the beginning of summer through to fall. Since it grows well in very sandy, poor soil, it is an excellent addition to a scree garden.

HAREBELL

Height: 1'
Color: Blue-purple
Bloom Time: Late spring through late summer
Light: Full sun to part shade
Soil: Sand, loam
Moisture: Dry to medium
Germination: CMS
Excellent in containers 10" or deeper
Not Everlasting
Not Deer Resistant
Not Salt Tolerant
Not Edible
Pollination Partners: Harebell is frequented by many small- to medium-sized bee species and many small butterflies. The seeds are too small to be of interest to any birds.
Native to:
  USA (AK, AZ, CA, CO, CT, IA, ID, IL, IN, MA, MD, ME, MI, MN, MO, MT, NC, ND, NE, NH, NJ, NM, NY, OH, OR, PA, SD, TN, TX, UT, VA, VT, WA, WI, WV, WY)
  CAN (AB, BC, LB, MB, NB, NF, NS, NT, NU, ON, PE, QC, SK, YT)

Lanceleaf/Sand Coreopsis ⚘ *Coreopsis lanceolata*

Long blooming *Coreopsis lanceolata* self-sows like the dickens, resulting in a riot of early summer color. A large, round-faced yellow flower set upon a long, thin stem looks fragile, but you will find that it lasts a surprising seven to ten days when cut. It is drought-tolerant, blooming from early to mid-summer, and can tolerate some shade. They work well in large swaths if you're looking for brilliant color in a particular area. You can extend the blooming season by deadheading for a second and even third blooming cycle.

LANCELEAF COREOPSIS/SAND COREOPSIS

Height: Height: 1' - 2'
Color: Yellow
Bloom Time: Early summer through late summer
Light: Full sun
Soil: Sand, loam, clay
Moisture: Dry to medium
Germination: NPT
Excellent in containers 12" or deeper
Not Everlasting
Deer Resistant
Salt Tolerant
Not Edible
Pollination Partners: Long- and short-tongued bees, wasps, flies, moths, beetles and butterflies (including many kinds of skippers) are attracted to the nectar. Clever Coreopsis also distributes its seeds with the barbs of the seed shells that attach themselves to the animal fur and human clothing.
Native to:
USA (AL, AR, CA, CO, CT, DE, FL, GA, HI, IA, IL, IN, KS, KY, LA, MA, MD, ME, MI, MN, MO, MS, NC, NE, NH, NJ, NM, NY, OH, OK, OR, PA, RI, SC, TN, TX, VA, VT, WA, WI, WV, WY)
CAN (BC, ON)

Spiderwort ❧ *Tradescantia ohiensis*

Spiderwort works hard to produce flowers beginning in late spring and ending early summer. The purple flowers open in the morning and close by early afternoon. They are not a long-lasting plant, having set seed by mid-summer. This plant is a great example of why you should not give wildflowers too much water, fertilizer, great soil or other high maintenance attention. To spoil Spiderwort is to encourage it to run rampant through your garden, becoming a floppy, disheveled mess late in the season. Best to leave Spiderwort to its own devices. The blue flowers taste like cucumber and look stunning in salads! Spiderworts are ravishing in a fresh cut arrangement and tend to last nicely for five to ten days.

SPIDERWORT

Height: 2' - 4'
Color: Blue
Bloom Time: Late spring through summer
Light: Full sun to part shade
Soil: Sand, loam, clay
Moisture: Dry to medium
Germination: CMS
Grows well in containers 12" or deeper
Not Everlasting
Not Deer Resistant
Not Salt Tolerant
Edible: flowers
Pollination Partners: Attracts honey bees, bumblebees, and native sweat bees as well as syrphid flies.
Native to:
 USA (AL, AR, CT, DE, FL, GA, IA, IL, IN, KS, KY, LA, MA, MD, ME, MI, MN, MO, MS, NC, NE, NH, NJ, NY, OH, OK, PA, RI, SC, TN, TX, VA, WI, WV)
 CAN (ON)

Late Spring - Early Summer
THE LEGUME FAMILY: WYNKEN, BLYNKEN AND POD

Look closely at the foliage on any Baptisia plant and something is likely to look very familiar to you. Their leaves bear a striking resemblance to Sweet Pea foliage! Blue False Indigo, White False Indigo, Yellow Wild Indigo, Purple Prairie Clover, Wild Senna and Wild Lupine are all in the same large legume family of plants that produce pods. Note: the wildflowers in this family do not produce edible pods! However, wildflowers in the legume family are extraordinarily beautiful and perform essential services to both the soil in your garden and the pollinators in your neighborhood.

Surely one of nature's secret weapons, legumes manufacture their own fertilizer, as well as fertilizer for neighboring plants! Organic farmers use well-known legumes, such as alfalfa and clover, to add nitrogen to their fields. Wildflowers in the legume family have deep, wide roots that plunge six to ten feet into the soil, opening pathways, encouraging earthworms and attracting healthy soil microbes that process decayed plant material into nutrient-rich soil.

Blue False/Wild Blue Indigo ❦ *Baptisia australia*

Although slow to establish, Wild Blue Indigo is long-lived. It is easy to grow from seed and adds interest in the garden throughout the growing season. This dramatic plant bursts forth out of the ground in spring with lightning speed. Bearing a striking resemblance to asparagus on steroids, Blue False Indigo soon produces clusters of dark indigo blue, lupine-like flowers on long stems in the early summer enhanced with blue-ish, gray/green foliage that is striking when used in floral arrangements. This plant grows well in full sun or partial shade. It also has a very deep taproot, so don't transplant it once it's been established. The blue spikes will easily last five to seven days in an arrangement. Baptisia's foliage, though sadly inconsistent in its staying power, is brilliant to use if you need it to last only 24 hours.

BLUE FALSE INDIGO/WILD BLUE INDIGO

Height: 2' - 5'
Color: Blue
Bloom Time: Late spring through early summer
Light: Full sun to part shade
Soil: Sand to loam
Moisture: Medium
Germination: CMS
Does not grow well in containers
Everlasting: Seed pods/natural maracas
Deer Resistant
Salt Tolerant
Not Edible
Pollination Partners: Queen bumblebees are important pollinators of the flowers. Other long-tongued bees may visit the flowers occasionally. It hosts orange sulphur, clouded sulphur, frosted elfin, eastern tailed blue, hoary edge and wild indigo duskywing butterflies. Poisonous leaves keep animals at bay.
Native to:
 USA (AL, AR, CT, DC, GA, IA, IL, IN, KS, KY, MA, MD, MI, MO, NC, NE, NH, NJ, NY, OH, OK, PA, SC, TN, TX, VA, VT, WI, WV)
CAN (ON)

Purple Prairie Clover ❧ *Dalea purpurea*

The bright purple and gold capsule-shaped flowers of Purple Prairie Clover appear in mid-summer. Dramatic when planted with Butterflyweed, Black-Eyed Susan and short prairie grasses, this important legume adds nitrogen to the soil naturally, so no fertilizer is necessary! Very drought-tolerant due to its deep taproot, it grows on most well-drained soils from dry sand to clay. It is a true show stopper in fresh and dried arrangements!

PURPLE PRAIRIE CLOVER

Height: 1' - 3'
Color: Purple
Bloom Time: Mid-summer
Light: Full sun
Soil: Sand, loam and clay
Moisture: Dry to medium
Germination: NPT
Grows well in containers 12" or deeper
Everlasting
Deer Resistant
Salt Tolerant
Not Edible
Pollination Partners: The flowers attract many kinds of insects, including every sort of bee imaginable! Purple Prairie Clover is reasonably tasty and high in protein; therefore, animals, with the exception of deer, eat this plant readily. Because it's so popular with animals, this plant can be difficult to establish in some areas if there is an abundance of grazing wildlife! Tiny rodents aid in distributing Purple Prairie Clover seeds when they carry the seeds to their dens. Grouse, pheasants, quails and pigeons relish the seed! It also attracts songbirds.

Native to:

USA (AL, AR, AZ, CO, GA, IA, IL, IN, KS, KY, LA, MI, MN, MO, MS, MT, ND, NE, NM, NY, OH, OK, SD, TN, TX, WI, WY)

CAN (AB, MB, ON, SK)

Quick to germinate in the spring, White False Indigo is also a survivor, being one of the longest living wildflowers. Growing quickly as soon as the ground unthaws, they can grow up to four feet in one month. Plants are easily recognized with small white popcorn-like flowers bursting off tall purple stems.

Like the other Baptisia plants, White Wild Indigo blooms from the bottom upwards and has exceedingly deep taproots that extend over ten feet down into the soil. These stunning plants require three to five years to produce flowers but are well worth the wait! The flowers are elegant and long-lived in fresh arrangements; the seed pods will naturally dry on the plant to form funky black pods. Shake them, and you've got a natural maraca!

WHITE FALSE INDIGO/WILD WHITE INDIGO

Height: 3' - 5'
Color: White
Bloom Time: Late spring through early summer
Light: Full sun to part shade
Soil: Sand, loam, clay
Moisture: Dry to medium
Germination: CMS
Does not grow well in containers
Everlasting: Seed pods/ natural maracas
Deer Resistant
Not Salt Tolerant
Not Edible
Pollination Partners: Worker and queen bumblebees pollinate wild white indigo flowers by wrestling open the blossoms. Caterpillars of skippers and butterflies feed on the leaves. It hosts orange sulphur, clouded sulphur, frosted elfin, eastern tailed blue, hoary edge and wild indigo duskywing butterflies. White Wild Indigo is poisonous, so is not readily eaten by animals.
Native to:
  USA (AL, AR, FL, GA, IA, IL, IN, KS, KY, LA, MI, MN, MO, MS, NC, NE, NY, OH, OK, SC, TN, TX, VA, WI)

Wild Lupine/Sundial Lupine ❦ *Lupinus perennis*

Springtime stars, Wild Lupine blossoms have dense spires of deep blue flowers on upright spikes. They have deep taproots, too, so they resent being transplanted. With distinctive foliage that's still far more subtle than showy Russell hybrid lupines, Wild Lupines are no visual slouch! I love using the blossoms in spring arrangements. The blossoms will last quite nicely for three to six days.

WILD LUPINE/SUNDIAL LUPINE
Height: 1' - 2'
Color: Blue
Bloom Time: Late spring through early summer
Light: Full sun to part shade
Soil: Sand, loam
Moisture: Dry to medium
Germination: SC
Grows well in containers 12" or deeper
Not Everlasting
Deer Resistant
Not Salt Tolerant
Not Edible
Pollination Partners: The flowers are cross-pollinated by honey bees, bumblebees and other long-tongued bees. Wild Lupine differs from other flowers because it's not passive during pollination. It forcibly ejects pollen into the faces of insect visitors! Karner Blue and other butterflies will visit in search of nectar. Other animals such as sheep and horses don't visit the plant, since the foliage is toxic to them.
Native to:
 USA (AL, CT, DC, DE, FL, GA, IA, IL, IN, KY, LA, MA, MD, ME, MI, MN, MS, NC, NH, NJ, NY, OH, PA, RI, SC, TX, VA, VT, WI, WV)
 CAN (NF, ON)

Wild Senna ❧ *Senna hebecarpa*

Wild Senna looks like an escapee from the tropics! Each year I am amazed to see such a large, exotic creature thriving in my Canadian garden. Large, feathery leaves accent tall yellow flowers. Wild Senna's chocolate-colored seed pods keep the show going well into fall. The giant, puffball, yellow flowers look amazing in fresh cut arrangements and last five to eight days.

WILD SENNA

Height: 4' - 6'
Color: Yellow
Bloom Time: Mid-summer
Light: Full sun to part shade
Soil: Sand, loam, clay
Moisture: Medium to moist
Germination: CMS
Dramatic by itself in large container at least 2' deep
Not Everlasting
Deer Resistant
Not Salt Tolerant
Not Edible
Pollination Partners: Sweat bees and bumblebees visit the flower for pollen. The caterpillars of some sulphur butterflies rely on Wild Senna foliage for food. Grazing mammals do not eat the plant because the foliage upsets their digestion. Seeds are eaten by game birds such as Bobwhite Quails and pheasants. Attracts songbirds.
Native to:
USA (CT, DC, DE, GA, IL, IN, KY, MA, MD, ME, MI, NC, NH, NJ, NY, OH, PA, RI, SC, TN, VA, VT, WI, WV)
CAN (ON)

Yellow False Indigo ⚘ *Baptisia sphaerocarpa*

I love the vivid yellow spikes of Yellow False Indigo! The plant forms bush-like clumps and deep taproot systems, so it shouldn't be disturbed after the first year it's planted. Sporting distinctive grey, green and blue leaves and stems, Yellow False Indigo's bright yellow flowers last for five to eight days in fresh arrangements. The flowers morph into handsome, chocolate brown, round seed pods (up to 3/4" diameter) that look stunning in dried flower arrangements.

YELLOW FALSE INDIGO

Height: 2' - 3'
Color: Yellow
Bloom Time: Late spring through early summer
Light: Full sun to part shade
Soil: Sand, loam, clay
Moisture: Dry to medium
Germination: CMS
Does not grow well in containers
Everlasting: Seed pods/natural maracas
Deer Resistant
Not Salt Tolerant
Not Edible
Pollination partners: This is a popular flower for many native bees, including the leaf-cutter and carpenter bee. *Baptisia sphaerocarpa* is also visited by monarch butterflies, smaller species of butterflies and large bees, such as the bumblebee.
Native to: (AR, LA, MO, MS, OK, TX)

Late Spring – Early Summer
THE BLACK-EYED SUSAN FAMILY

Black-Eyed Susans are like apple pie – we all love them! Long-blooming and easy to grow, every single member of the Rudbeckia family has showy, daisy-shaped yellow or gold flowers with yummy chocolate-colored centers. All Rudbeckia species make superb cut flowers, with the seed heads giving texture and earthiness to an arrangement. What's not to love?

Black-Eyed Susan  *Rudbeckia hirta*

Black-Eyed Susans are biennials, but if you didn't know that beforehand, you will think I'm making it up; they self-sow like crazy, creating the illusion of a perennial. They are a no-brainer addition to any garden, since they are salt-resistant, drought- and clay-tolerant and grow in the poorest of soil qualities. Get ready for bright yellow blooms that last throughout most of the summer. Superb as long-lasting, fresh cut flowers, I also enjoy air drying them upside down for a natural-looking, super-wild effect in everlasting arrangements.

BLACK-EYED SUSAN

Height: 1'- 3'
Color: Yellow
Bloom Time: Late spring through early fall
Light: Full sun to part shade
Soil: Sand, loam, clay
Moisture: Dry to medium
Germination: NPT
Excellent in containers 10" or deeper
Everlasting
Deer Resistant
Salt Tolerant
Not Edible
Pollination Partners: Many pollinators find Black-Eyed Susans appealing. Sweat bees, mining bees, wasps and butterflies collect pollen or suck on nectar. Some butterfly larvae consume leaves. Mammals are not fond of the hairy, coarse leaves. Goldfinches enjoy the seeds.
Native to:
USA (AK, AL, AR, CA, CO, CT, DC, DE, FL, GA, IA, ID, IL, IN, KS, KY, LA, MA, MD, ME, MI, MN, MO, MS, MT, NC, ND, NE, NH, NJ, NM, NY, OH, OK, OR, PA, RI, SC, SD, TN, TX, UT,VA, VT, WA, WI, WV, WY)
CAN (AB, BC, MB, NB, NF, NS, ON, PE, QC, SK)

A true perennial, this cousin of the Black-Eyed Susan is a long-lived and long-blooming flower with fuzzy leaves. If you look closely, the central cone of the flower head gives off a shimmering appearance. Growing three to six feet in height, it is taller and has larger blossoms than the common Black-Eyed Susan. This plant makes for a superb, long-lasting cut flower.

SWEET BLACK-EYED SUSAN

Height: 3 ' - 6'
Color: Yellow
Bloom Time: Late summer through fall
Light: Full sun to part shade
Soil: Sand, loam, clay
Moisture: Medium to moist
Germination: CMS
Excellent in containers 1.5' or deeper
Not Everlasting
Not Deer Resistant
Not Salt Tolerant
Not Edible
Pollination Partners: Well-utilized by a wide range of pollinators seeking nectar including long- and short-tongued bees, wasps, butterflies and beetles. Occasionally, beetles feed on the pollen. Their rough leaves make Sweet Black-Eyed Susan unappealing to animal foragers.
Native to:
  USA (AR, CT, IA, IL, IN, KS, KY, LA, MA, MI, MO, MS, NC, NY, OK, TN, TX, WI)

57

The Heart of Summer

In the peak of summer, I've been known to wander for hours, drunk with happiness, through my wildflower gardens and meadows. Everywhere I look, nature's beauty jumps up to greet me. Obvious – and not so obvious – vignettes of beauty and pollinator interaction are everywhere. Butterflies, exotic wasps and bumblebees dance among thousands of wildflowers and native grasses.

Over the years, I have built many traditional, high-maintenance gardens filled with annuals, hybrid perennials or vegetables. But as far as I'm concerned, nothing beats the beauty and ease of a wildflower garden in mid-summer. If you wish to bother, you can deadhead the Gaillardia and Coreopsis so they rebound later in the summer. That's it, though. No watering or fertilizing; only observation, flower arranging and joy!

Bergamot/Beebalm ❧ *Monarda fistulosa*

Highly fragrant, this unusual-looking member of the mint family grows well in sunny, open fields and woodland borders. Aromatic purple flowers attract a large number of bees, as well as some butterfly species. Bergamot does spread by rhizomes, so you will notice its clumping behavior. Stems may be used by some bird species to build nests. The flowers are excellent for fresh cut bouquets that last 4 to 6 days and make a great minty tea.

BERGAMOT/BEEBALM

Height: 2' - 5'
Color: Lavender
Bloom Time: Mid-summer through late summer
Light: Full sun to part shade
Soil: Sand, loam, clay
Moisture: Dry to medium
Germination: NPT
Grows well in containers 1.5' or deeper
Not Everlasting
Deer Resistant
Not Salt Tolerant
Edible: flowers
Pollination Partners: The nectar of the flowers attracts honey bees, bumblebees and other long-tongued bees. Sometimes, sweat bees collect pollen, and some wasps steal nectar by puncturing the nectar tube. Butterflies will visit occasionally but are not fruitful beebalm pollinators. Ruby-Throated Hummingbirds also visit the flowers. Mammalian herbivores do not enjoy the oregano-mint flavor of the leaves, which also cause indigestion in these animals.
Native to:
USA (AL, AR, AZ, CO, CT, DC, DE, GA, IA, ID, IL, IN, KS, KY, LA, MA,MD, ME, MI, MN, MO, MS, MT, NC, ND, NE, NH, NJ, NM, NV, NY, OH, OK, OR, PA, RI, SC, SD, TN, TX, UT,VA, VT, WA, WI, WV, WY)
CAN (AB, BC, MB, NT, ON, QC, SK)

Blue Vervain ❀ *Verbena hastata*

Native to the wetter areas (marshes, sloughs, pond edges), this plant will grow five to six feet tall and will produce blue flower spikes in its second year. The seeds are best sown on open, rich soil. Blue Vervain is a must in a meadow-style garden with medium to moist soil or an old-fashioned English cottage-style garden. Blue Vervain's spiky purple glow absolutely thrills me in fresh cut flower arrangements. They will last five to eight days as fresh cut flowers.

BLUE VERVAIN

Height: 2' - 5'
Color: Blue
Bloom Time: Mid-summer through late summer
Light: Full sun to part shade
Soil: Sand, loam, clay
Moisture: Medium to moist
Germination: CMS
Grows well in containers 1.5' or deeper
Not Everlasting
Not Deer Resistant
Salt Tolerant
Not Edible
Pollination Partners: The flowers attract long- and short-tongued bees, including epoline cuckoo bees, eucerin miner bees, sweat bees, oligolege bees and the *Calliopsis verbenae* (verbena bee). Other pollinators include wasps, flies, small butterflies, skippers and beetles. Verbena moth caterpillars like to eat the foliage. Sparrows and juncos will eat the seed.
Native to:
  USA (AL, AR, AZ, CA, CO, CT, DC, DE, FL, GA, IA, ID, IL, IN, KS, KY, LA, MA, MD, ME, MI, MN, MO, MS, MT, NC, ND, NE, NH, NJ, NM, NV, NY, OH, OK, OR, PA, RI, SC, SD, TN, TX,UT, VA, VT, WA, WI, WV, WY)
  CAN (BC, MB, NB, NS, ON, QC, SK)

Cardinal Flower ❧ *Lobelia cardinalis*

Absolutely treasured in the garden, the brilliant red spires of the Cardinal Flower will bloom for a month or longer. The Cardinal Flower is very particular about its location and needs moist, rich soil in partial shade. Be warned, however, because even professional gardeners find that it will often not make it through a winter. This isn't because of the cold, but because the plant is particularly sensitive to the freeze-thaw action of early spring and therefore may need replanting in the spring. The plant is definitely worth it, even if just to attract the hummingbirds! Cardinal Flowers make stunning cut flowers that will last from three to five days in the vase.

CARDINAL FLOWER

Height: 2' - 5'
Color: Red
Bloom Time: Mid-summer through late summer
Light: Full sun to part shade
Soil: Sand, loam
Moisture: Medium to moist
Germination: CMS
Grows well in containers 12" or deeper
Not Everlasting
Deer Resistant
Not Salt Resistant
Not Edible
Pollination Partners: Ruby-Throated Hummingbirds and swallowtail butterflies are attracted to this flower and will drink the nectar. Bumblebees are also common visitors, sometimes slitting open the tubular blossom to reach the nectar inside. Birds don't eat the tiny seeds, and white latex in the plant's foliage protects it from being eaten by mammalian herbivores.
Native to:
USA (AL, AR, AZ, CA, CO, CT, DC, DE, FL, GA, IA, IL, IN, KS, KY, LA, MA, MD, ME, MI, MN, MO, MS, NC, NE, NH, NJ, NM, NV, NY, OH, OK, PA, RI, SC, TN, TX, UT, VA, VT, WI,WV)
CAN (NB, ON, QC)

Common Evening Primrose ❧ *Oenothera biennis*

The flowers of the Common Primrose are short-lived, opening at dusk and closing by noon the next day. Flowering primarily at night makes pollinators highly specialized, and in fact, survival of the Common Primrose depends on night-thriving moths. Native to dry meadows and now found along roadsides, this plant tolerates a range of conditions. Early settlers in North America grew the plant for its nutritious roots. The buds, blossoms and seedpods all make interesting additions to summer and fall bouquets.

COMMON EVENING PRIMROSE
Height: 2' - 6'
Color: Yellow
Bloom Time: Late spring through summer
Light: Full sun to part shade
Soil: Sand, loam, clay
Moisture: Dry to moist
Germination: NPT
Does not grow well in containers
Everlasting Seed Pods
Not Deer Resistant
Salt Tolerant
Not Edible
Pollination Partners: Moths pollinate Common Evening Primrose, especially sphinx moths. Other pollinators include the Ruby-Throated Hummingbird, honey bees and bumblebees. Caterpillars of several kinds of moths like to feed on the foliage, and goldfinches eat the plant's seeds. Attracts songbirds.
Native to:
 USA (AL, AR, CA, CT, DC, DE, FL, GA, IA, IL, IN, KS, KY, LA, MA,MD, ME, MI, MN, MO, MS, MT, NC, ND, NE, NH, NJ, NM, NV, NY, OH, OK, OR, PA, RI, SC, SD, TN, TX, VA, VT,WA, WI, WV)
 CAN (AB, BC, MB, NB, NF, NS, ON, PE, QC, SK)

Culver's Root ❧ *Veronicastrum virginicum*

Easily identifiable from a distance, Culver's Root produces elegant white spires that float above the garden or meadow. The plant grows well in any medium-to-moist soil in full sun or part shade and their spikes add drama to any fresh flower arrangement.

CULVER'S ROOT

Height: 3' - 6'

Color: White

Bloom Time: Mid-summer through late summer

Light: Full sun to part shade

Soil: Sand to clay

Moisture: Medium to moist

Germination: NPT

Grows well in containers 1.5' or deeper

Not Everlasting

Not Deer Resistant

Not Salt Tolerant

Not Edible

Pollination partners: The most common visitors to the flowers are long- and short-tongued bees, collecting pollen and nectar, including honey bees, bumblebees and mason bees. Other kinds of insect visitors include wasps, butterflies, moths and flies. The seeds are too tiny to be of much interest to birds.

Native to:

USA (AL, AR, CT, DC, DE, FL, GA, IA, IL, IN, KS, KY, LA, MA, MD, ME, MI, MN, MO, MS, NC, ND, NE, NJ, NY, OH, OK, PA, SC, SD, TN, TX, VA, VT, WI, WV)

CAN (MB, NS, ON)

Dotted Mint/Spotted Beebalm ⚜ *Monarda punctata*

I'm pretty sure you've never seen anything like the Dotted Mint. Looking at the photo here, your first impression may be, "Wow! Look at those pretty pink flowers!" In fact, you'd be mistaken: those pink "flowers" aren't flowers at all. Rather, they are the leaves surrounding the true flowers that bloom every other year (biennial). Quite an aromatic plant, it is frequented by many butterfly species. It also makes an excellent addition to any bouquet or arrangement, lasting four to six days.

DOTTED MINT/SPOTTED BEEBALM

Height: 1' - 2'
Color: Pink
Bloom Time: Mid-summer through early fall
Light: Full sun
Soil: Sand, loam
Moisture: Dry to medium
Germination: NPT
Grows well in containers 12" or deeper
Not Everlasting
Deer Resistant
Not Salt Tolerant
Not Edible
Pollination Partners: The nectar and pollen attracts bumblebees and honey bees. The endangered Karner blue butterfly is attracted to the nectar. The oregano-scented foliage and flowers are unattractive to mammalian herbivores. Attracts hummingbirds.
Native to:
 USA (AL, AR, CA, CT, DC, DE, FL, GA, IA, IL, IN, KS, KY, LA, MA, MD, MI, MN, MO, MS, NC, NJ, NM, NY, OH, OK, PA, SC, TN, TX, VA, VT, WI)
 CAN (ON, QC)

Great Blue Lobelia *Lobelia siphilitica*

Great Blue Lobelia, the blue counterpart of the Cardinal Flower, prefers moist soils and can be found naturally in open, moist, shaded woodlands and alongside lakes and streams. Longer lived than the Cardinal Flower and far less fussy about where it grows, Great Blue Lobelia blooms in late summer, producing spikes of deep blue flowers and attracting hummingbirds. This plant self-sows to create even more beautiful blue spikes! Excellent for damp clay soils, it is a great addition to any garden with that soil type. Great Blue Lobelia also makes a reasonably sturdy cut flower that lasts three to five days in the vase.

GREAT BLUE LOBELIA
Height: 1' - 4'
Color: Blue
Bloom Time: Mid-summer through early fall
Light: Full sun to part shade
Soil: Sand, loam, clay
Moisture: Medium to moist
Germination: CMS
Excellent in containers 12" or deeper
Not Everlasting
Not Deer Resistant
Not Salt Tolerant
Not Edible
Pollination Partners: Great Blue Lobelia is frequented by honey and native bees for pollen. Butterflies and moths visit for nectar, which also attracts hummingbirds.
Native to:
USA (AL, AR, CO, CT, DC, DE, GA, IA, IL, IN, KS, KY, LA, MA, MD, ME, MI, MN, MO, MS, NC, ND, NE, NH, NJ, NY, OH, OK, PA, SC, SD, TN, TX, VA, VT, WI, WV, WY)
CAN (MB, ON)

Hoary Vervain *Verbena stricta*

A true star in the wildflower cutting garden, Hoary Vervain is an extremely drought-resistant plant that naturally occurs in dry, sandy soils. Producing long, lavender-colored flower stalks, it stands out in any planting. It blooms throughout the heat of the summer, lasting for many weeks. An absolute knockout in fresh arrangements!

HOARY VERVAIN

Height: 2' - 4'
Color: Blue
Bloom Time: Early summer through late summer
Light: Full sun
Soil: Sand to loam
Moisture: Dry to medium
Germination: CMS
Grows well in containers 1.5' or deeper
Not Everlasting
Deer Resistant
Salt Tolerant
Not Edible
Pollination Partners: Attracts many bee species, including miner bees, green metallic bees, honey bees, bumblebees, carpenter bees, leaf-cutting bees and cuckoo bees. Some caterpillars eat the foliage, while their adult moth and butterfly counterparts help to pollinate. Attracts songbirds.
Native to:
  USA (AL, AR, AZ, CO, CT, DE, GA, IA, ID, IL, IN, KS, KY, MA, MI, MN, MO, MS, MT, NC, ND, NE, NJ, NM, NV, NY, OH, OK, PA, SD, TN, TX, UT, VT, WA, WI, WV, WY)
  CAN (ON, QC)

Ironweed ❧ *Vernonia fasciculata*

Ironweed's velvety, textured, purple flowers are impossible to ignore in the summer and early fall garden. A hardy perennial, it can tolerate moist to medium soils, and its height brings color to the back of any border. Ironweed was the very first wildflower I experimented with as a cut flower. It did not disappoint! Ironweed's purple velvet punch is stunning in fresh arrangements, lasting seven to ten days.

IRONWEED

Height: 4' - 6'
Color: Purple
Bloom Time: Mid-summer through early fall
Light: Full sun to part shade
Soil: Sand, loam, clay
Moisture: Medium to moist
Germination: CMS
Grows well in containers 1.5' or deeper
Not Everlasting
Deer Resistant
Not Salt Tolerant
Not Edible
Pollination Partners: The nectar is useful to bee flies, butterflies, skippers and long-tongued bees. The caterpillars of various moths feed on the stems and roots of Ironweeds. Because of its bitter leaves, animals will not eat Ironweed.
Native to:
 USA (AR, CO, IA, IL, IN, KS, KY, MA, MN, MO, MS, MT, ND, NE, NY, OH, OK, SD, TX, WI)
 CAN (MB)

Lavender Hyssop/Licorice Hyssop ❧ *Agastache foeniculum*

I have a great deal of affection for Lavender Hyssop. I never get tired of taking a leaf off a plant in the nursery or the garden, crumpling it up to release the scent, and then handing pieces around to the assembled group, asking, "Do you recognize that smell?" Everyone gets a faraway look in their eyes as they race through their scent memory files. Always one bold individual pronounces the scent to be licorice, and everyone smiles. Lavender Hyssop, a member of the mint family, makes a superb tea. The flowers have a licorice flavor that is said to benefit the digestion. Steep 2-3 tablespoons of bruised fresh leaves and several flowers in two cups of boiled water for five minutes; strain and drink hot or iced.

LAVENDER HYSSOP/LICORICE HYSSOP

Height: 1' - 3'
Color: Lavender
Bloom Time: Mid-summer through late summer
Light: Full sun to part shade
Soil: Sand, loam, clay
Moisture: Dry to medium
Germination: NPT
Grows well in containers 1.5' or deeper
Everlasting
Deer Resistant
Not Salt Tolerant
Edible: leaves and flowers
Pollination Partners: This plant is super popular with pollinators! The flowers are cross-pollinated by honey bees, bumblebees, digger bees, leaf-cutting bees, sweat bees and masked bees – Other occasional floral visitors are various flies, butterflies, skippers and moths. This plant also attracts hummingbirds. Animals do not like the taste or smell of licorice, however, so they avoid Lavender (or Licorice) Hyssop. This plant is edible, so be sure to enjoy it in teas, salads, soups, cookies – anywhere the taste of anise or licorice would be appreciated.
Native to:
  USA (CO, CT, DE, IA, IL, KY, MI, MN, MT, ND, NE, NH, NY, PA, SD, WA, WI, WY)
  CAN (AB, BC, MB, NB, NT, ON, QC, SK)

Mountain Mint ❦ *Pycnanthemum virginianum*

Clusters of white blossoms contrast well with the glossy dark green foliage of this plant. When adding this to your garden, be sure to take the time to appreciate the great mint aroma. Treasured by bee keepers, Mountain Mint also attracts butterflies and hummingbirds. The delicate white flowers are lovely to include in herbal arrangements.

MOUNTAIN MINT

Height: 2' - 3'
Color: White
Bloom Time: Spring through summer
Light: Full sun to part shade
Soil: Sand, loam, clay
Moisture: Medium to moist
Germination: NPT
Grows well in containers 12" in depth or greater
Not Everlasting
Deer Resistant
Not Salt Tolerant
Not Edible
Pollination Partners: Many insects will pollinate the flowers, including bees, wasps, flies, small butterflies and beetles seeking nectar. Animals do not like the minty taste and rarely will eat this plant.
Native to:
  USA (AL, AR, CT, DE, GA, IA, IL, IN, KS, KY, MA, MD, ME, MI, MN, MO, MS, NC, ND, NE, NH, NJ, NY, OH, OK, PA, RI, SD, TN, VA, VT, WI, WV)
  CAN (NB, ON, QC)

Nodding Wild Onion ❦ *Allium cernuum*

In addition to offering visual charm in any garden or vase, this accommodating native onion also plays a tasty supportive role in salads, soups and sautées. Its green stems may be used like scallions in all forms of cooking.

NODDING WILD ONION

Height: 1' - 2'
Color: white/pink
Bloom Time: Mid-summer through early fall
Light: Full sun to part shade
Soil: Sand to loam
Moisture: Dry to medium
Germination: SC
Grows well in containers 10" in depth or greater
Not Everlasting
Deer Resistant
Not Salt Tolerant
Edible: Entire plant
Pollination Partners: Short-tongued bees in the Halictidae family (sweat bees) are attracted to the purple flowers. You may see flies in the Syrphidae family (syrphid flies) frequently visit the plant, but only to forage for nectar – they are not prolific pollinators of the Nodding Wild Onion.
Native to:
  USA (AL, AR, AZ, CO, DC, GA, IA, ID, IL, IN, KY, MD, MI, MN, MO, MS, MT, NC, NE, NM, NY, OH, OR, PA, SC, SD, TN, TX, UT, VA, WA, WI, WV, WY)
  CAN (AB, BC, ON, SK)

Rattlesnake Master ✽ *Eryngium yuccifolium*

This unusual, bizarrely handsome plant attracts attention in the landscape. Transforming from blue to silver as they mature, the thistle-like heads will add varying color to your garden all season long. The spiky flowers are supported by tall, thin stalks whose roots reach deep into the ground. It is important to note that this plant does not transplant well after becoming established in the first year. The dried seed heads were used as rattles by native North Americans. Rattlesnake Master received its attention-grabbing name because pioneers mistakenly thought its roots could be used as a cure for rattlesnake bites. A long-lived cut flower, Rattlesnake Master works beautifully in large, dramatic arrangements or as an enhancement in soft, intimate bouquets, lasting 8 to15 days.

RATTLESNAKE MASTER

Height: 2 '- 4'
Color: White
Bloom Time: Mid-summer through fall
Light: Full sun
Soil: Sand, loam, clay
Moisture: Dry to medium
Germination: CMS
Grow well by themselves in containers 2' in depth or more
Not Everlasting
Deer Resistant
Not Salt Tolerant
Not Edible
Pollination Partners: The flowers bring many kinds of insects, including long-tongued bees, short-tongued bees, wasps, flies, butterflies, skippers, moths, beetles, and plant bugs. The rough leaves and sharp flowers hold no interest for animals.
Native to:
  USA (AL, AR, CT, FL, GA, IA, IL, IN, KS, KY, LA, MD, MI, MN, MO, MS, NC, NE, NJ, OH, OK, SC, TN, TX, VA, WI)

I adore Artemisia! This aromatic plant is a superb drought-tolerant ground cover for medium to dry landscapes. The entire plant has silver-colored foliage, which makes its colorful neighbors pop in a garden or a bouquet. Called "man sage" by native peoples, this plant was often used in ceremonies. Because it spreads its silvery self by rhizomes, be sure to plant it where its ever-expanding silvery beauty will be appreciated and not cause problems for other plants.

SILVER SAGE/SILVER KING

Height: 1' - 2'
Color: Silver
Bloom Time: Summer through fall
Light: Full sun to part shade
Soil: Sand, loam, clay
Moisture: Dry to medium
Germination: NPT
Excellent by itself in container 1' or deeper
Everlasting
Deer Resistant
Not Salt Tolerant
Not Edible

Pollination Partners: The flowers don't attract insects because they are wind pollinated, but several grasshopper species feed on the foliage of Silver Sage. Mammalian herbivores don't eat *Artemisia ludoviciana* because the bitter taste repulses them, and the seeds are too small to be of much interest to birds.

Native to:
USA (AR, AZ, CA, CO, CT, DE, FL, GA, IA, MD, ME, MI, MN, MO, MS, MT, NC, ND, NE, NH, NJ, NM, NV, NY, OH, OK, OR, PA, RI, SC, SD, TN, TX, UT, VA, VT, WA, WI, WY)
CAN (AB, BC, MB, NB, NT, ON, PE, QC, SK)

Sweet Joe-Pye Weed ❦ *Eupatorium purpureum*

One of the taller wildflowers in wooded areas, Sweet Joe-Pye Weed is easily grown. It has numerous tiny, vanilla-scented, pinkish/purple flowers grouped into huge, dome-shaped umbels. These flower bunches act like magnets for monarchs, swallowtails and many other butterflies. The plant's textured leaves are attractive all season long. This is an excellent garden plant, and like Joe-Pye Weed, it contributes greatly to fresh flower arrangements and bouquets.

SWEET JOE-PYE WEED

Height: 3' - 6'
Color: Pink
Bloom Time: Mid- through late summer
Light: Full sun to part shade
Soil: Sand, loam, clay
Moisture: Medium to moist
Germination: CMS
Grows well in containers 1.5' or deeper
Not Everlasting
Deer Resistant
Not Salt Tolerant
Not Edible
Pollination Partners: The flower nectar attracts primarily bumblebees and other long-tongued bees, butterflies, skippers and moths. Some bees also collect pollen. The Swamp Sparrow eats the seeds of various Joe-Pye Weeds to a limited extent.
Native to:
 USA (AL, AR, CT, DC, DE, FL, GA, IA, IL, IN, KS, KY, LA, MA, MD, ME, MI, MN, MO, MS, NC, NE, NH, NJ, NY, OH, OK, PA, RI, SC, TN, VA, VT, WI, WV)
 CAN (ON)

White Yarrow ❦ *Achillea millefolium*

Trusty, soft-colored, long-blooming and oh-so-dainty, *Achillea millefolium* will be your friend forever. This well-known native looks glorious when planted in cream colored swaths in the garden. White Yarrow does spread by rhizomes, so be sure to plant it in an area where it can spread out. The feathery, fern-like foliage and wide, flat heads of *Achillea millefolium* look gorgeous in fresh and dried bouquets!

WHITE YARROW

Height: 1' - 2'
Color: White
Bloom Time: Summer
Light: Full sun, part shade
Soil: Sand, loam, clay
Moisture: Dry to medium
Germination: NPT
Grows well in containers 1' or deeper
Everlasting
Deer Resistant
Salt Tolerant
Not Edible
Pollination Partners: The nectar of the flowers attracts many kinds of insects, especially flies, wasps, and sweat bees who also collect pollen. Several species of grasshoppers feed on White Yarrow, and so do the caterpillars of some moth species. Because the foliage of yarrow has a bitter taste, it's not popular among mammalian herbivores, except for sheep, which don't seem to mind the taste.
Native to:
USA (AK, AL, AR, AZ, CA, CO, CT, DC, DE, FL, GA, HI, IA, ID, IL, IN, KS, KY, LA, MA, MD, ME, MI, MN, MO, MS, MT, NC, ND, NE, NH, NJ, NM, NV, NY, OH, OK, OR, PA, RI, SC, SD,TN, TX, UT, VA, VT, WA, WI, WV, WY)
CAN (AB, BC, LB, MB, NB, NF, NS, NT, NU, ON, PE, QC, SK, YT)

Wild Quinine ⚜ *Parthenium integrifolium*

I am head over heels in love with Wild Quinine. Sophisticated and sturdy, Wild Quinine plays a starring role in many of my garden and floral designs. The tiny white flowers form flat white blooms that last all summer long. Its rich neutral color combines beautifully with any type of flower and foliage you choose.

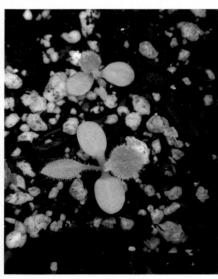

WILD QUININE
Height: 2' - 5'
Color: White
Bloom Time: Late spring to summer
Light: Full sun to part shade
Soil: Sand, loam, clay
Moisture: Dry to medium
Germination: CMS
Grows well in containers 1.5' or deeper
Everlasting
Deer Resistant
Not Salt Tolerant
Not Edible
Pollination Partners: Sweat bees, wasps, flies, and beetles appear to be attracted to the flowers with beetles preferring pollen and others, the nectar. The beetles feed on pollen and the other insects feed on nectar. Rough leaves with a bitter taste keep mammals away.
Native to:
  USA (AL, AR, CT, GA, IA, IL, IN, KS, KY, LA, MA, MD, MI, MN, MO, MS, NC, NY, OH, OK, PA, SC, TN, TX, VA, WI, WV)

The Heart of Summer

THE MILKWEED FAMILY

Milkweeds are an essential larval food source for monarch butterflies and a group of insects that specialize in eating plants with very powerful chemical defence systems. They are also an important nectar source for bees.

Milkweeds are heavily predated upon by butterfly and moth larva (caterpillars), but to avoid serious damage, they have specialized defence mechanisms: cardiac glycosides, latex fluids, and leaf hairs. Monarch butterflies have evolved with milkweed making them able to ingest the toxins with no negative outcomes. These toxins build up in their bodies effectively making them poisonous to birds.

Milkweeds have a brilliant pollination system. Pollen sacs attach to the feet of visiting insects when they land on notches in the flowers. The sacs are then carried off by pollinators to cross-pollinate other flowers.

Milkweed species grow seeds in pods that contain silk or floss. When the seeds ripen, the pods burst open and the seeds float off in the wind.

Butterflyweed/Butterfly Milkweed *Asclepias tuberosa*

Butterflyweed is strikingly beautiful with its seemingly impossible orange blossoms that appear mid-summer. Aptly named for its ability to attract a range of butterfly partners, Butterflyweed will grow to three feet in height. Requiring warm soil makes it slow to start but bloom time coordinates well with the appearance of adult butterflies. This relatively low-growing wildflower has deep taproots so you have about one year to change your mind about where it lives in your garden! Stunning in bouquets, it will last nicely in an arrangement for three to six days. The seed pods are gorgeous to use in fresh and dried arrangements. If you want to use the pods, douse them with hair spray to prevent them from bursting open.

BUTTERFLYWEED/BUTTERFLY MILKWEED

Height: 2' - 3'
Color: Orange
Bloom Time: Early through late summer
Light: Full sun to part shade
Soil: Sand to loam
Moisture: Dry to medium
Germination: CMS
Does not grow well in containers
Everlasting: Seed Pods
Deer Resistant
Salt Tolerant
Not Edible
Pollination Partners: The nectar of Butterflyweed flowers attracts long-tongued bees, sphecid wasps and various butterflies, including swallowtails and fritillaries. The Ruby-Throated Hummingbird also seeks nectar from the flowers. Because it is a type of milkweed, the monarch caterpillars' food of choice, this plant is often munched on by the caterpillars.
Native to:
USA (AL, AR, AZ, CA, CO, CT, DC, DE, FL, GA, IA, IL, IN, KS, KY, LA, MA, MD, ME, MI, MN, MO, MS, NC, NE, NH, NJ, NM, NY, OH, OK, PA, RI, SC, SD, TN, TX, UT, VA, VT, WI,WV)
CAN (ON, QC)

Common Milkweed ❧ *Asclepias syriaca*

Common Milkweed produces a profusion of sweet-scented, spherical, soft pink flowers and is the primary food source for the caterpillars of the monarch butterfly. Spreading easily by rhizomes, this flower is best planted with other wildflowers and native grasses to avoid its rapid spread outside of where you'd prefer it to be. Nature has combined mine with our asparagus patch – a really beautiful look! I like to use the milkweed pods in fresh arrangements for a dramatic, earthy effect. If you wish to use the pods in dried arrangements, make sure to coat them in hair spray to keep the pods from bursting open.

COMMON MILKWEED

Height: 2' - 3'
Color: Lavender
Bloom Time: Early summer through mid-summer
Light: Full sun
Soil: Sand, loam, clay
Moisture: Dry to medium
Germination: CMS
Does not grow well in containers
Everlasting: Seed Pods
Deer Resistant
Not Salt Tolerant
Not Edible
Pollination Partners: Visitors to milkweed plants include long-tongued bees, wasps, flies, skippers and butterflies looking for nectar. The caterpillars of the monarch butterfly frequent the plant, as they feed on the foliage. Other insect visitors include short-tongued bees, various milkweed plant bugs and moths, including sphinx moths.
Native to:
  USA (AL, AR, CT, DC, DE, GA, IA, IL, IN, KS, KY, LA, MA, MD, ME, MI, MN, MO, MS, MT, NC, ND, NE, NH, NJ, NY, OH, OK, OR, PA, RI, SC, SD, TN, TX, VA, VT, WI, WV)
CAN (MB, NB, NS, ON, PE, QC, SK)

Red Milkweed/Swamp Milkweed ❧ *Asclepias incarnata*

Red Milkweed will win you over with its pink blossoms and captivating fragrance. Artfully designed to be a landing pad for monarchs, these beauties are naturally found in low-lying areas at the edge of swamps and ponds. Their blossoms are flat, rich clusters of flowers ranging from a deep, rose-purple color to pale rose. These lovely flowers are enhanced with an intoxicating fragrance that combines cinnamon, vanilla and honey. Red Milkweed is beautiful outside the house and in, and you will be thrilled with its appearance and longevity in floral arrangements! If you wish to use the seed pods in dried arrangements, it's best to douse them in hair spray to keep them from bursting open.

RED MILKWEED/SWAMP MILKWEED

Height: 3' - 5'
Color: Pink/Red
Bloom Time: Summer
Light: Full sun to part shade
Soil: Sand, loam, clay
Moisture: Medium to moist
Germination: CMS
Does not grow well in containers
Everlasting: Seed Pods
Deer Resistant
Not Salt Tolerant
Not Edible
Pollination Partners: The nectar of Red Milkweed is very popular with many kinds of pollinators, including bumblebees, honey bees, sweat bees, various wasps, flies, swallowtail butterflies, greater fritillaries, monarch butterflies, skippers and the occasional Ruby-Throated Hummingbird. Animals will not eat this plant because the leaves contain cardiac glycosides, which is toxic.
Native to:
USA (AL, AR, CO, CT, DC, DE, FL, GA, IA, ID, IL, IN, KS, KY, LA, MA, MD, ME, MI, MN, MO, MT, NC, ND, NE, NH, NJ, NM, NV, NY, OH, OK, PA, RI, SC, SD, TN, TX, UT, VA, VT, WI,WV, WY)
CAN (MB, NB, NS, ON, PE, QC)

The Heart of Summer

THE ECHINACEA FAMILY

There is something utterly irresistible about coneflowers! They are extremely easy to grow from seed, look smashing in the garden and make superb cut flowers. These tough, drought-tolerant plants attract beneficial wildlife and can handle very cold temperatures.

Most Echinacea species have large, fleshy taproots that search for moisture and nutrients. Purple Coneflower is the exception, with much shallower roots than its relatives. The genus is named after the Greek word for hedgehog, echinos, because the center of the flower is prickly.

Overall, these versatile, hardy plants make great additions to any garden or bouquet.

Ozark Coneflower ❧ *Echinacea paradoxa*

Ozark Coneflowers are rare, native wildflowers found only in the Ozark region of Arkansas and Missouri, although they are actually quite hardy. With a gigantic seed head and long, thin, bright yellow petals, these Coneflowers have an almost comical look. Easily hybridized, the Ozark Coneflower is often responsible for the abnormally-colored Coneflowers that are so popular today. Ozark Coneflower looks tremendous in fresh flower arrangements and last moderately well as a cut flower, staying fresh for an average of four to seven days.

OZARK CONEFLOWER

Height: 3' - 4'
Color: Yellow
Bloom Time: Early through late summer
Light: Full sun
Soil: Sand, loam, clay
Moisture: Medium
Germination: CMS
Grows well in containers 1.5' or deeper
Not Everlasting
Not Deer Resistant
Not Salt Tolerant
Not Edible
Pollination Partners: The most fragrant of all coneflowers attracting bumble and honey bees but is particularly attractive to butterflies, especially the regal fritillary. The Ozark Coneflower also attracts songbirds.
Native to:
  USA (AR, MO, OK, TX)

Pale Purple Coneflower *Echinacea pallida*

Imagine what the love child of a Purple Coneflower and the long-necked brontosaurus dinosaur might look like! If it existed, it would look like the Pale Purple Coneflower. Like an awkward teenager, Pale Purple Coneflower's large purple coneheads and gangly pink petals make it look a little unwieldy, but these disproportionate flowers make for early summer drama in the garden. Easily one to two feet taller than the Purple Coneflower and blooming a month earlier, these long-blooming flowers are followed by dramatic seed coneheads that provide texture and shape all season long. Pale Purple Coneflower forms deep taproots when mature, so its location in your garden cannot be changed after one year. Pale Purple Coneflower lasts well in fresh cut arrangements and looks beautiful growing in the garden.

PALE PURPLE CONEFLOWER

Height: 2' - 5'
Color: Pink/purple
Bloom Time: Early summer through mid-summer
Light: Full sun to part shade
Soil: Sand, loam, clay
Moisture: Dry to medium
Germination: CMS
Grows well in containers 2' or deeper
Not Everlasting
Deer Resistant
Salt Tolerant
Not Edible
Pollination Partners: Butterflies, bumblebees and skippers are the most useful visitors to the flowers. Seeds attract goldfinshes; foliage attracts some livestock although other food sources are preferred.
Attracts songbirds.
Native to:
USA (AL, AR, CT, GA, IA, IL, IN, KS, LA, MA, MD, ME, MI, MO, NC, NE, NY, OK, SC, TN, TX, VA, WI)
CAN (ON)

Purple Coneflower ❦ *Echinacea purpurea*

Perhaps best known and beloved of wildflowers, this robust, drought-tolerant perennial is a top-notch pollinator attractor! Blooming profusely for up to two months in the summer, the showy flowers are arranged individually on sturdy stems. Soft purple petals surround a funky-textured, iridescent, red-orange, cone-shaped center. Purple Coneflower performs beautifully in cut flower arrangements and remains fresh for up to ten days.

PURPLE CONEFLOWER

Height: 2' - 4'
Color: Purple
Bloom Time: Mid-summer through fall
Light: Full sun to part shade
Soil: Sand, loam, clay
Moisture: Dry to medium
Germination: CMS
Grows well in containers 1.5' or deeper
Not Everlasting
Deer Resistant
Salt Tolerant
Not Edible
Pollination Partners: The flowers are pollinated by long-tongued bees and sweat bees. Bee flies are also attracted to the Purple Coneflower. Butterfly pollinators include monarchs, fritillaries, painted ladies, swallowtails and members of the Coliadinae and Pieridae families. The caterpillars of the silvery checkerspot butterfly will eat the leaves, and the Eastern Goldfinch eats the seeds.
Native to:
USA (AL, AR, CO, CT, FL, GA, IA, IL, IN, KS, KY, LA, MD, MI, MO, MS, NC, NJ, NY, OH, OK, PA, SC, TN, TX, VA, WI, WV)
CAN (ON)

Tennessee Coneflower ❧ *Echinacea tennesseensis*

Once considered a truly rare native plant, the Tennessee Coneflower has made a comeback – and it's no wonder! Thought to be nearing extinction in the 1960's, this coneflower variety was saved after its beguiling upright dark pink petals won the hearts of many. The dark pink blooms are different from other coneflowers in that the petals are horizontal rather than drooping, and the cone is a greenish/pink color. Tennessee Coneflower is compact, vigorous and exceptionally long blooming in the garden. It also makes a superb, long-lasting cut flower that lasts 6-10 days.

TENNESSEE CONEFLOWER
Height: 1' - 2'
Color: Pink/purple
Bloom Time: Early summer through fall
Light: Full sun
Soil: Sand to loam
Moisture: Medium
Germination: CMS
Grows well in containers 1.5' or deeper
Not Everlasting
Deer Resistant
Not Salt Tolerant
Not Edible
Pollination Partners: Tennessee Coneflower is often visited by honey bees, many species of large and small native bees, moths and many butterfly species, particularly skippers. It also attracts songbirds.
Native to:
 USA (TN)

Yellow/Gray-Head Coneflower ❦ *Ratibida pinnata*

An honorary member of the coneflower family, Yellow Coneflower is a summer-blooming thrill and a superb choice for the wildflower garden or meadow. Its droopy, vivid yellow blooms last for such a long time! The tall stems are extremely thin, causing it to sway and flutter in the breeze, much like a decorative native grass. Mid-summer, Yellow Coneflower's snappy-looking yellow and green buds are long-lasting in arrangements. The bright petals of the full bloom will not last longer than two days in an arrangement.

YELLOW CONEFLOWER/GRAY-HEAD CONEFLOWER

Height: 3' - 6'
Color: Yellow
Bloom Time: Mid-summer into early fall
Light: Full sun to part shade
Soil: Sand, loam, clay
Moisture: Dry to moist
Germination: CMS
Grows well in containers 1.5' or deeper
Not Everlasting
Not Deer Resistant
Not Salt Tolerant
Not Edible
Pollination Partners: Many insects visit the flowers, but especially sweat bees. Other insect visitors include wasps, flies, small butterflies and beetles that suck nectar from the flowers. Particularly, Yellow Coneflower attracts silvery checkerspot caterpillars and several species of moth caterpillars. Goldfinches eat the seeds, and groundhogs and livestock enjoy eating the foliage and flowering stems. Attracts songbirds.
Native to:

USA (AL, AR, CT, FL, GA, IA, IL, IN, KS, KY, LA, MA, MI, MN, MO, MS, NE, NJ, NY, OH, OK, PA, SC, SD, TN, VA, VT, WI, WV)
CAN (ON)

The Heart of Summer

THE SILPHIUM SOCIETY

The Silphium family is an acquired taste! These towering members of the sunflower family have sandpaper-like leaves and bright yellow blossoms. Their pine-scented resinous sap was used as chewing gum by pioneers; cattle and buffalo will eat the entire plant to the ground.

Silphiums have developed some rather unique survival strategies. Their rough leaves deter insects and help conserve water. Left undisturbed, silphiums can grow to a height of ten feet or more, then die back and begin again the next year. Aldo Leopold, the beloved naturalist, had a deep respect for the plant: "Silphiums first became a personality to me when I tried to dig one up to move it to my farm. The root was like a great vertical sweet potato." Silphium roots grow downward to depths of ten to fifteen feet in order to weather prairie droughts. Their presence in wildflower gardens and meadows lends dramatic flair to the landscape.

Compass Plant ❦ *Silphium laciniatum*

The young Compass Plant resembles a two-foot-tall oak tree, with leaves that tend to point north/south (which is how pioneers came to name this ancient prairie plant). Amerindian children used its resin as a chewing gum! Once it is established, Compass Plant is not easily moved, thanks to an enormous taproot. As it matures (albeit, fairly slowly), you will find that each plant produces more flowers, sometimes up to a hundred per month. Despite their enormous height, Compass Plants rarely flop over because their thick stems hold them erect through all sorts of extreme weather. I enjoy using their bright green buds and vivid yellow flowers in summer arrangements. They will last five to eight days in the vase.

COMPASS PLANT

Height: 3' - 10'
Color: Yellow
Bloom Time: Early summer through early fall
Light: Full sun
Soil: Sand, loam, clay
Moisture: Dry to medium
Germination: CMS
Does not grow well in containers
Not Everlasting
Not Deer Resistant
Not Salt Tolerant
Not Edible
Pollination Partners: Bumblebees and other long-tongued bees are the primary pollinators. Sulphur butterflies and monarchs occasionally visit the flowers for nectar. Goldfinches enjoy eating the seeds.
Native to:
  USA (AL, AR, CO, DC, IA, IL, IN, KS, KY, LA, MI, MN, MO, MS, ND, NE, NM, NY, OH, OK, PA, SD, TN, TX, VA, WI)
  CAN (ON)

Cup Plant ❧ *Silphium perfoliatum*

Eccentric, quirky and the life of the wildflower garden party, Cup Plants have so much going for them! The plant grows eight to ten feet tall with sturdy square stems and sports large pointed leaves that form a cup that birds and butterflies often will drink. Cup Plants are perfect as a natural summertime privacy fence. In the fall, the seeds are a goldfinch favorite. The blooms and buds add flare to both large and small arrangements and last for five to eight days.

CUP PLANT

Height: 3' - 8'
Color: Yellow
Bloom Time: Early summer into fall
Light: Full sun to part shade
Soil: Sand, loam, clay
Moisture: Medium to moist
Germination: CMS
Does not grow well in containers
Not Everlasting
Not Deer Resistant
Not Salt Tolerant
Not Edible
Pollination Partners: Long-tongued and short-tongued bees, butterflies, skippers and wasps tend to pollinate the flowers. Various birds, especially goldfinches are very fond of the seeds and drink water from the cup-shaped leaves. Dense colonies provide shelter for the goldfinches. Attracts hummingbirds   .
Native to:
  USA (AL, AR, CT, GA, IA, IL, IN, KS, KY, LA, MA, MD, ME, MI, MN, MO, MS, NC, ND, NE, NJ, NY, OH, OK, PA, SD, TN, VA, VT, WI, WV)
  CAN (ON, QC)

The ancient cousin of Compass and Cup Plants, Prairie Dock grows eight to ten feet tall and sports cheery yellow flowers. Prairie Dock produces elongated, almost tropical leaves that resemble elephant's ears, extending upwards toward the bright yellow flowers. It prefers rich clay soils with good moisture, but it also does well on fertile, well-drained land. Like others in the Silphium family, its bright green flower buds look tremendous in arrangements, and so do the bright yellow flowers, lasting five to ten days.

PRAIRIE DOCK/PRAIRIE ROSINWEED
Height: 3' - 10'
Color: Yellow
Bloom Time: Mid- to late summer
Light: Full sun
Soil: Sand, loam, clay
Moisture: Medium to moist
Germination: CMS
Does not grow well in containers
Not Everlasting
Not Deer Resistant
Not Salt Tolerant
Not Edible
Pollination Partners: Long- and short-tongued bees, butterflies, skippers and wasps will visit the flowers. Various birds, especially goldfinches, relish the seeds.
Native to:
  USA (AL, AR, DC, GA, IA, IL, IN, KY, MI, MO, MS, NC, OH, SC, TN, VA, WI, WV)
  CAN (ON)

The Heart of Summer

THE BLAZINGSTAR FAMILY

To know one blazingstar is to love all blazingstars. Easy to grow from seed, each Liatris plant creates a corm that expands to grow more and more pollinator-attracting purple spikes. Corms resemble bulbs, except they look more like woody nuggets. The corm is actually a dormant stem that comes to life each spring and blooms in late summer.

These magical wands of purple beauty bloom from the top down and make superb fresh cut flowers, as well as long-lasting dried flowers. Budding Liatris spikes provide great texture and color to fresh arrangements.

Meadow Blazingstar 🌿 *Liatris ligulistylis*

Unlike other Blazingstar varieties, Meadow Blazingstar's brilliant purple flowers are numerous and widely-branched. This extraordinary plant is also a monarch magnet and is unsurpassed in attracting the beloved butterflies. It is also an excellent food source for goldfinches. Meadow Blazingstar makes a dramatic fresh flower that blooms for 5 to 8 days and then transforms easily into a stunning dried flower, so don't limit it to just blooming in your garden. If you have medium to moist soil, please consider growing this important plant to support the dwindling monarch butterfly population.

MEADOW BLAZINGSTAR

Height: 3' - 5'
Color: Purple/Pink
Bloom Time: Mid-summer through late summer
Light: Full sun
Soil: Loam
Moisture: Medium
Germination: CMS
Excellent in containers 1'or deeper
Everlasting
Not Deer Resistant
Not Salt Tolerant
Not Edible
Pollination Partners: Honey bees, bumblebees and other long-tongued bees, butterflies and skippers visit the flowers. Like Rough Blazingstar, Meadow Blazingstar is often home to the caterpillars of the rare glorious flower moth, which feeds on the flowers and seed capsules. Rabbits, deer, groundhogs and livestock all eat the foliage and stems, and small rodents will occasionally dig up the corms and eat them. This plant also attracts songbirds and hummingbirds.
Native to:
  USA (CO, CT, IA, IL, MN, MO, MT, ND, NM, SD, WI, WY)
  CAN (AB, MB, SK)

Prairie Blazingstar ❧ *Liatris pycnostachya*

The tallest of the Blazingstar family, Prairie Blazingstar, like its brethren, is very attractive to monarch butterflies. Partial to moist areas and thrilled to grow in pure clay, Prairie Blazingstar looks like a giant purple fairy wand and is a great cut flower lasting 5 to 8 days. It also holds its color well in dried flower arrangements.

PRAIRIE BLAZINGSTAR

Height: 2' - 5'
Color: Purple/pink
Bloom Time: Mid- to late summer
Light: Full sun
Soil: Sand, loam, clay
Moisture: Dry to moist
Germination: CMS
Grows well in containers 1' or deeper
Everlasting
Deer Resistant
Salt Tolerant
Not Edible
Pollination Partners: The flowers are pollinated by honey bees, bumblebees, other long-tongued bees, butterflies and skippers. Butterflies such as monarchs, swallowtails, painted ladies, sulphurs and whites also pollinate the plant. Just like other Liatris, Prairie Blazingstar is a choice food for the glorious flower moth, whose caterpillars feed on the flowers and seed capsules. Small rodents sometimes eat the corms. This plant also attracts songbirds and hummingbirds.
Native to:
  USA (AR, IA, IL, IN, KS, KY, LA, MA, MI, MN, MO, MS, ND, NE, NJ, NY, OH, OK, PA, SD, TX, WI)

93

Rough Blazingstar ❦ *Liatris aspera*

Rough Blazingstar is the latest blooming of the Liatris. This plant is for you if you long to grow *Liatris* but think you can't because your soil is too sandy and dry. Other *Liatris* need medium to moist soils, but *Liatris aspera* loves dry, poor soil. *Liatris aspera* makes a superb cut flower, both in its early bud form as an attractive spike and when it comes into bloom in late summer.

ROUGH BLAZINGSTAR
Height: 2' - 3'
Color: Purple/pink
Bloom Time: Late summer through early fall
Light: Full sun
Soil: Sand, loam
Moisture: Dry
Germination: CMS
Grows well in containers 1' or deeper
Everlasting
Not Deer Resistant
Not Salt Tolerant
Not Edible
Pollination Partners: Honeybees, bumblebees and other long-tongued bees, butterflies and skippers visit the flowers. The caterpillars of the glorious flower moth eat the flowers and seed capsules of Rough Blazingstar and other Liatris. Large and small mammals like to eat the foliage and stems, including rabbits, deer, groundhogs and livestock. Occasionally, small rodents will dig up the corms and eat them. Songbirds are also attracted to the plant.
Native to:
 USA (AL, AR, FL, GA, IA, IL, IN, KS, KY, LA, MI, MN, MO, MS, NC, ND, NE, NY, OH, OK, SC, SD, TN, TX, VA, WI, WV)
 CAN (ON)

The Heart of Summer

THE WILD SUNFLOWER FAMILY

When I first fell in love with wildflowers, I was thrilled to learn about perennial wild sunflowers. Perennial wild sunflower blooms attract many of the same insects as annual sunflowers, including long-tongued and short-tongued bees, butterflies, skippers and beetles.

Also, just like annual wildflowers, the seeds of perennial wild sunflowers are an attractive food source to both birds and small mammals. And you don't have to grow these bright yellow beauties from seed over and over again every year!

Downy Sunflower ❧ *Helianthus mollis*

I am extremely partial to Downy Sunflower, but I must warn you that this tough sunflower forms dense colonies in poor or stony soil. It spreads by rhizomes, and I like to let it meander around my gardens because I love the look. This rare sunflower has soft, gray/green leaves and buds that produce an abundance of large, buttercup yellow flowers in late summer. Its strong stems are highly valued by finches and many other birds. I use the striking silver foliage and buds as filler and as an accent in arrangements and bouquets all summer. Then in late summer, the bright flowers create a wow factor for any bouquet, lasting 4-6 days.

DOWNY SUNFLOWER

Height: 2' - 4'
Color: Yellow
Bloom Time: Late summer through early fall
Light: Full sun
Soil: Sand to loam
Moisture: Dry to medium
Germination: CMS
Grow well by themselves in large container 2' or deeper
Not Everlasting
Not Deer Resistant
Not Salt Tolerant
Not Edible
Pollination Partners: Bees, including bumblebees and sweat bees, are the primary visitors to the flowers for nectar or pollen. The caterpillars of silvery checkerspot butterflies feed on the foliage. The seeds are popular with many kinds of birds, ground squirrels and other small rodents. Songbirds are attracted to the plant, and goldfinches especially love the seeds.
Native to:
USA (AL, AR, CT, GA, IA, IL, IN, KS, KY, LA, MA, MD, ME, MI, MO, MS, NC, NE, NJ, NY, OH, OK, PA, RI, SC, TN, TX, VA, WI, WV)
CAN (ON)

Ox-Eye Sunflower/False Sunflower ❧ *Heliopsis helianthoides*

Not a true sunflower but a beloved imposter, Ox-Eye Sunflowers are a true workhouse in the wildflower garden, meadow or vase. Found naturally in tall grass prairies at the edge of brushy or wooded areas, these long-blooming wonders are a non-stop summer source of long-lasting cut flowers that stay fresh for 4 to 5 days. .

OX-EYE SUNFLOWER/FALSE SUNFLOWER

Height: 2' - 5'
Color: Yellow
Bloom Time: Early summer through late summer
Light: Full sun to part shade
Soil: Sand, loam, clay
Moisture: Dry to medium
Germination: CMS
Grows well in containers 1.5' or deeper
Not Everlasting
Not Deer Resistant
Not Salt Tolerant
Not Edible
Pollination Partners: Insects such as long-tongued bees, sweat bees, bee flies and butterflies are all attracted to the nectar and pollen of the flowers. Songbirds also enjoy the plant, and many species of birds enjoy eating the seeds.
Native to:
 USA (AL, AR, CO, CT, DC, DE, FL, GA, IA, IL, IN, KS, KY, LA, MA, MD, ME, MI, MN, MO, MS, NC, ND, NE, NH, NJ, NM, NY, OH, OK, PA, RI, SC, SD, TN, TX, VA, VT, WA, WI, WV)
 CAN (MB, NB, NF, ON, QC, SK)

The Fall Families

If you don't love the glorious textures and colors of the fall wildflower garden or meadow – you're off your rocker! Asters and goldenrods, ironweeds and native grasses glow with color. Achingly gorgeous seed pods of Baptisia, Coneflowers, Gaillardia and Liatris accent the rich color, texture and movement of the fall wildflower garden.

Native grasses come in many shapes, sizes and behaviors. Some are as low-growing as a foot tall, while others grow eight feet tall. Some are clump-forming and polite, slowly creating a wider and wider clump. Other grasses will spread to form luxurious swaths. Native grasses not only provide beauty in gardens and meadows, but they perform some rather impressive landscaping maintenance services as well: they shelter young wildflower plants from severe heat so they can grow big and strong; and they work with wildflowers to block weeds from invading a garden or meadow. The bittersweet beauty of the fall garden reaches a crescendo after the first hard frost, when many native grasses transform into orange or dusty pink masses waving in the wind. I urge you…please don't tidy up your garden until spring. The fall and winter garden provides shelter and sustenance to all creatures in your landscape's ecosystem. Enjoy the shapes and forms of dormant wildflowers and native grasses. They are a comforting reminder that spring will come again. You will notice that the grasses do not have a Pollinator Partner category. Grasses are wind pollinated or they propagate through rhizomal action (travelling roots). Grasses, however, do provide important functions within the animal community so you will see a new category specifically for grasses titled, Ecosystem Partners.

New England Aster ❦ *Symphyotrichum novae-angliae*

A real workhorse in the fall garden, New England Aster has bright purple or pink petals and sunny yellow centers. Naturally occurring in moist areas, this is one of the showiest of all the asters. It produces clusters of large flowers at the end of numerous branching stems, ranging from pink to deep purple petals and distinct yellow-orange centers. A late-season nectar source for a variety of butterflies, I love using New England Asters in richly colored fall arrangements. They will last for three to five days.

NEW ENGLAND ASTER

Height: 3' - 6'
Color: Pink/purple
Bloom Time: Late summer through mid fall
Light: Full sun to part shade
Soil: Sand, loam, clay
Moisture: Medium to moist
Germination: CMS
Grows well in containers 1.5' or deeper
Not Everlasting
Deer Resistant
Salt Tolerant
Not Edible
Pollination Partners: The flowers are pollinated by long-tongued bees, bee flies, butterflies and skippers. Short-tongued bees and flies will collect pollen.
Native to:
USA (AL, AR, CA, CO, CT, DC, DE, GA, IA, IL, IN, KS, KY, MA, MD, ME, MI, MN, MO, MS, MT, NC, ND, NE, NH, NJ, NM, NY, OH, OK, OR, PA, RI, SC, SD, TN, UT, VA, VT, WA, WI,WV, WY)
CAN (BC, MB, NB, NS, ON, QC)

Showy Goldenrod  *Solidago speciosa*

Showy Goldenrod is a clump-forming, extremely polite member of the Solidago family. I find this species to be the most attractive of all the goldenrods, with its strong yellow spires of tiny flowers. A great addition to fall arrangements, both fresh and dried.

SHOWY GOLDENROD

Height: 1'- 4'
Color: Yellow
Bloom Time: Late summer through mid fall
Light: Full sun to part shade
Soil: Sand, loam
Moisture: Dry to medium
Germination: CMS
Grow well by themselves in large containers 2' or deeper
Everlasting
Not Deer Resistant
Salt Tolerant
Not Edible
Pollination Partners: The flowers mostly attract honey bees, bumblebees, ants and beetles seeking nectar. The caterpillars of many moths feed on this goldenrod and others. Attracts songbirds.
Native to:
  USA (AR, CO, CT, GA, IA, IL, IN, KS, KY, LA, MA, MD, MI, MN, MO, MS, NC, ND, NE, NH, NJ, NM, NY, OH, OK, PA, RI, SC, SD, TN, TX, VA, VT, WI, WV, WY)
  CAN (MB, ON)

Sky Blue Aster ❧ *Symphyotrichum oolentangiense*

Shhhh! Don't tell anyone, but Sky Blue Aster is my absolute favorite aster. And I'll tell you why–Sky Blue Aster doesn't shout that fall is coming. Sky Blue Aster blooms are a subtle, glowing blue that startle you as you stroll through the garden. Bunches of lavender/blue flowers with bright yellow centers appear to hover over brilliantly green leaves. They are a must-have for lasting color. Its arrow-shaped leaves are distinctive all season long. The soft blue blossoms look smashing in fall arrangements and last five to ten days.

SKY BLUE ASTER

Height: 2' - 3'
Color: Lavender blue
Bloom Time: Late summer through mid fall
Light: Full sun to part shade
Soil: Sand, loam
Moisture: Dry to medium
Germination: CMS
Grows well in containers 1' or deeper
Not Everlasting
Deer Resistant
Not Salt Tolerant
Not Edible
Pollination Partners: Popular with sweat bees, hummingbirds and butterflies, including many skippers. Attracts songbirds.
Native to:
  USA (AL, AR, FL, GA, IA, IL, IN, KS, LA, MI, MN, MO, MS, NC, NE, NY, OH, OK, SD, TN, TX, WI)
  CAN (ON)

Clumping and non-invasive, Stiff Goldenrod is an excellent addition for fall color in the garden and in both dried and fresh arrangements. This plant creates flattened flower heads, different from Showy Goldenrod, but grows similar small, yellow flowers. Throughout the summer, masses of the grey-green buds work beautifully in arrangements to add texture and fill space.

STIFF GOLDENROD

Height: 2' - 5'
Color: Yellow
Bloom Time: Late summer through early fall
Light: Full sun
Soil: Sand, loam, clay
Moisture: Dry to medium
Germination: CMS
Grows well in large containers 1.5' or deeper
Everlasting
Not Deer Resistant
Salt Tolerant
Not Edible
Pollination Partners: Stiff Goldenrod attracts many kinds of insects – long- and short-tongued bees, wasps, flies butterflies and beetles; monarch butterflies are especially attracted to the flowers. Goldfinches enjoy the seeds, and many mammals will eat this plant when no other food source is available. Attracts songbirds.
Native to:
  USA (AR, CT, DC, IA, IL, IN, KS, KY, LA, MA, MD, MI, MO, NC, NE, NY, OH, OK, PA, RI, SC, TN, TX, VA, WI, WV)
  CAN (ON)

Big Bluestem ❧ *Andropogon gerardii*

Considered the great granddaddy of native grasses, majestic Big Bluestem once covered thousands of miles from the Atlantic Ocean to the Rocky Mountains. Big Bluestem commands attention with its four to eight foot height. Like most native grasses this grass is in its glory in late summer and early fall. During the shoulder season between summer and fall I use Big Bluestem in large, lush arrangements where its beautiful blue-green blades and turkey claw-shaped bloom lend color, texture and movement to a bouquet. Thriving on a tremendous range of soils, the green of the leaves and stems changes with the first frost to an attractive reddish-copper color that provides landscape interest well into winter.

BIG BLUESTEM
Height: 4' - 8'
Color: Green/bronze
Bloom Time: Late summer through late fall
Light: Full sun
Soil: Sand, loam, clay
Moisture: Dry to moist
Germination: NPT
Excellent by itself in container 1.5' or deeper
Not Everlasting
Deer Resistant
Not Salt Tolerant
Not Edible
Ecosystem Partners: Big Bluestem provides sustenance for many pollinators including butterflies and buffalo. Seeds are enjoyed by many sparrows.
Native to:
  USA (AL, AR, AZ, CO, CT, DC, DE, FL, GA, IA, IL, IN, KS, KY, LA, MA, MD, ME, MI, MN, MO, MS, MT, NC, ND, NE, NH, NJ, NM, NY, OH, OK, PA, RI, SC, SD, TN, TX, UT, VA, VT, WI,WV, WY)
  CAN (MB, ON, QC, SK)

Little Bluestem ❧ *Schizachyrium scoparium*

Little bluestem grass is the queen of versatility in the garden and vase! Its stunning blue, green and purple blades give any garden or meadow a sophisticated look. A patch of Little Bluestem waving in the wind is a beautiful sight. It is short and mixes well with many wildflowers. In fall and winter, the beauty continues as Little Bluestem changes to a soft, almost indescribable pink that emits a subtle glow.

LITTLE BLUESTEM

Height: 2' - 3'
Color: Green
Bloom Time: Late summer through late fall
Light: Full sun
Soil: Sand, Loam, clay
Moisture: Dry to medium
Germination: NPT
Excellent in large containers 1.5' or deeper
Not Everlasting
Not Deer Resistant
Salt Tolerant
Not Edible
Ecosystem Partners: Caterpillars of several skippers feed on the leaves and many grasshoppers feed on the foliage. Sparrows, juncos and other small songbirds eat the seeds, especially during winter. The foliage is quite desirable to bison, cattle and other hoofed mammals. Attracts songbirds
Native to:
 USA (AL, AR, AZ, CA, CO, CT, DC, DE, FL, GA, HI, IA, ID, IL, IN, KS, KY, LA, MA, MD, ME, MI, MN, MO, MS, MT, NC, ND, NE, NH, NJ, NM, NY, OH, OK, PA, RI, SC, SD, TN, TX, UT,VA, VT, WA, WI, WV, WY)
 CAN (AB, BC, MB, NB, NS, ON, QC, SK)

Prairie Dropseed ❀ *Sporobolus heterolepis*

A classy addition to any project, Prairie Dropseed is often used to create dramatic yet tidy borders (which is easily accomplished by planting about two feet apart). Subtly fragrant, described as cilantro meets popcorn, the seeds are ground by some Native peoples to make flour. Prairie Dropseed seed heads lend a note of gravitas to fresh arrangements.

PRAIRIE DROPSEED

Height: 2'
Color: Green
Bloom Time: Late summer through late fall
Light: Full sun
Soil: Sand, loam
Moisture: Dry to medium
Germination: NPT
Excellent in large containers 1.5' or deeper
Everlasting
Not Deer Resistant
Salt Tolerant
Not Edible
Ecosystem Partners: Caterpillars of the Leonard's Skipper feed on foliage and seeds are extremely nutritious fodder for a good number of songbirds including the Field, Savannah, and Tree Sparrow as well as the Slate-Colored Junco. Provides food for some livestock and is enjoyed by small rodents who burrow readily through the tufts.
Native to:
 USA (AR, CO, CT, GA, IA, IL, IN, KS, KY, MA, MD, MI, MN, MO, MT, NC, ND, NE, NM, NY, OH, OK, PA, SD, VA, WI, WY)
 CAN (MB, ON, QC, SK)

FOUR

Non-Native Must Haves

If you are looking for cheap thrills, you've come to the right place. Growing annuals is all about instant gratification, a satisfying hit of vivid color and the joy of tasty, tangible food on the table. I could just as soon stop breathing as stop growing annual heirloom flowers, herbs, everlastings and vegetables.

*　*　*

Feel free to boldly combine non-natives with natives in the garden – just as you should include wildflowers in your vegetable garden, your cutting garden or even your traditional flower border. Pollinators thrive on diversity.

Allow me to introduce my favorite non-native must-have annuals – starting with 4 beautiful edibles.

Celosia ❧ *Celosia argentea* and *celosia cristata*
Wool flowers, Cockscombs, Velvet flower, Lagos spinach, Feather flower, Mfungu (in Swahilii)

IF YOU ARE A COLOR JUNKIE, LIKE ME, YOU will want to grow Celosia. Their vivid color and bizarre, brain-like or feathery-plumed shapes are like an amusement park in the garden! And, if that's not enough of an incentive, Celosia leaves, young stems and inflorescences are edible, highly nutritious and taste like mild spinach. Celosia supplies a blast of color in the vase and dry beautifully.

CELOSIA

Height: 1' - 3'

Color: Mixed

Bloom Time: Mid-summer to fall

Light: Full sun

Soil: Rich loam

Moisture: Medium

Native to: Mexico, South America, Africa, West Indies, South and Central Asia

Annual

Everlasting

Edible

Chinese Basil   *Perilla frutescens* **var.** *crispa*
Shiso, Perilla, Beefsteak Plant, Purple perilla, Summer coleus, Wild basil

CHINESE BASIL
Height: 1' - 2'

Color: Mixed

Bloom Time: Mid-summer through fall

Light: Full sun

Soil: Loam or amended clay

Moisture: Dry to medium

Native to: India

Annual

Not Everlasting

Edible

FULL DISCLOSURE: I AM OBSESSED WITH Japanese food! I love everything about it – its nature-reverent aesthetics, the attention to detail and, most of all, the tastes. Originally from India, then China, but embraced by the Japanese back in the 9th century, shiso is an easy-to-grow annual. A member of the mint family, shiso, or perilla (or other names, above), has a unique taste and smell that is a cross between mint and indescribable. It has many health benefits, including a goodly amount of omega-3 oils. I add it to sushi rolls, rice and beans, tuna or tomato salad. In the garden, shiso provides rich green or purple swaths. Like basil, I use its massive spikes in fall bouquets.

Kale ❧ *Brassica oleracea*

KALE HAS A WELL-DESERVED REPUTATION as THE cool plant to grow and eat! I grow dark purple kale for drama in the garden, nutrition on the plate and beauty in the vase. Kale forms an elegant backdrop for brightly-colored flowers by making colors just pop. My purple kale responded well to the fish-composted soil. By the end of the summer the kale was over four feet tall!

KALE

Height: 1' – 4'

Color: Green/ purple

Bloom Time: Mid-summer through fall

Light: Full sun

Soil: Sand, loam, clay

Moisture: Dry to medium

Native to: Member of the cabbage family; originated in Mediterranean region

Annual

Not Everlasting

Edible

Scarlet Runner Bean ❧ *Phaseolus coccineus*

SCARLET RUNNER BEANS ARE DANCERS THAT gracefully wend their way through the garden, performing pirouettes among fellow flowers one day and reaching for the sky the next. Their bright red flowers are a marvel in the garden and vase! Their green pods are edible when immature, and the beans can be used fresh or dried. The starchy roots are still eaten by Central American Indians. I adore the look of their elegant spotted beans.

SCARLET RUNNER BEAN

Height: 2' - 8'

Color: Red

Bloom Time: Mid-summer to early fall

Light: Full sun

Soil: Rich

Moisture: Dry to medium

Native to: Mountains of Central America

Annual

Not Everlasting

Edible

Annual Statice ❧ *Limonium sinuatum*

ANNUAL STATICE

Height: 1' - 2'

Color: Mixed

Bloom Time: Mid-summer through fall

Light: Full Sun

Soil: Loam or amended clay

Moisture: Dry to medium

Native to: North Africa

Annual

Everlasting

Not Edible

WHEN DRIED FLOWERS WERE IN THEIR heyday in the 1980s, pretty much everyone knew or grew this brightly-colored everlasting. The more you harvest Statice, the more papery flowers it produces. If you want to dry the flower, harvest those with the widest possible blossom. I simply sneak a peek at the blossoms out of the corner of my eye. The blooms that catch my eye tend to have the widest, flattest blossoms and are ready for drying. Statice will dry upright in the vase or you can hang them up to dry. The mass of color is so very beautiful for interior décor. I have some hanging in my study. Statice also looks great displayed in bushel baskets or any deep, wide container.

Billy Buttons ❦ *Craspedia globosa*
Billy Balls, Woolly Heads, Drumstick Flower

THE PERFECTLY ROUND, GOLDEN YELLOW balls of Craspedia add color and shape to fresh and dried arrangements. In fact, they look so perfectly round and perky that it's easy to assume they are artificial! I find them delightfully absurd, and I enjoy growing them. I'm very pleased this everlasting of the '80s is once again being included in floral arrangements.

BILLY BUTTONS

Height: 1' - 1.5'

Color: Yellow

Bloom Time: Mid-summer through fall

Light: Full sun

Soil: Loam

Moisture: Dry to medium

Native to: Australia and New Zealand

Annual

Everlasting

Not Edible

Globe Amaranth ❦ *Gomphrena globosa*

GLOBE AMARANTH IS A TROPICAL ANNUAL with sturdy, clover-like, papery flowers that continually bloom throughout summer. They look like colorful buttons of red, purple, pink and white. Gomphrena flowers are so sturdy that they are commonly used in Hawaiian leis, since they retain their shape and color after drying. The reds become tallest. The more you harvest Globe Amaranth, the more it grows. Harvest the flowers when their heads are full and thick. They have firm stems so there is no need to dry them upside down. Use a bunch for a blast of color in fresh or dried bouquets. They look delightful hung upside down as everlasting décor.

GLOBE AMARANTH

Height: 1' - 2'

Color: Mixed

Bloom Time: Mid-summer through fall

Light: Full sun

Soil: Loam or amended clay

Moisture: Dry to medium

Native to: Brazil, Panama and Guatemala

Annual

Everlasting

Not Edible

Honeywort ❧ *Cerinthe major 'Purpurescens'*
Blue Shrimp Flower

I LIKE TO PLANT LOW-GROWING *CERINTHE* at the front of the border or to frame an entire bed. Their blossoms of soft blue and green are complex, subtle and elegant. *Cerinthe* blossoms stream like a fountain from a center stem so they lend a sophisticated, cascading quality to bouquets.

HONEYWORT

Height: 1' - 2'

Color: Blue

Bloom Time: Mid-summer through fall

Light: Full Sun

Soil: Loam or amended clay

Moisture: Dry to medium

Native to: Southern Europe

Annual

Not Everlasting

Not Edible

Kiss-me-over-the-garden-gate ❦ *Persicaria orientale*
Lady Fingers

KISS-ME-OVER-THE-GARDEN-GATE PLANTS ARE the drama queens of the cutting garden! With big, thick bamboo-like stems, a height of up to ten feet and cascading blossoms of hot pink chenille ropes, Kiss-me-over-the-garden-gate makes a superb privacy screen. A member of the knotweed family, this beauty self-sows with ease. The floppy, cascading look of the blossoms makes a dramatic contribution to both fresh and dried arrangements. I enjoy drying Kiss-me-over-the-garden-gate in the vase! When you bunch it and hang it upside down, it retains its shape!

KISS-ME-OVER-THE-GARDEN-GATE

Height: 2' - 10'

Color: Dark pink

Bloom Time: Summer through fall

Light: Full sun

Soil: Loam or amended clay

Moisture: Dry to medium

Native to: Eurasia

Annual

Everlasting

Not Edible

Larkspur ❧ *Consolida ambigua*
Annual Delphinium, Rocket Larkspur

THE LOVELY SPIKES OF LARKSPUR BLOOM from the bottom up. If you are harvesting for drying, harvest when the spikes are two-thirds in bloom. Larkspur's lush blossoms look stunning in fresh arrangements, dry easily and maintain their vivid color for a very long time. Larkspur germinates best in cooler winter temperatures, so spread the seed outside in late fall to germinate the following spring. You can also seed it in the spring indoors or outdoors at cool temperatures.

LARKSPUR

Height: 1' - 2.5'

Color: Mixed

Bloom Time: Mid-summer to summer

Light: Full sun

Soil: Rich soil

Moisture: Dry to medium

Native to: Western Europe, Mediterranean and Asia

Annual

Everlasting

Not Edible

Lemon Mint ❦ *Monarda citriodora*
Lemon Beebalm, Lemon Horsemint, Purple Horsemint

LEMON MINT

Height: 2' - 2.5'

Color: Mauve

Bloom Time: Mid-summer through fall

Light: Full sun

Soil: Loam or amended clay

Moisture: Dry to medium

Native to: Much of the United States and Mexico

Annual in cold climates

Everlasting

Not Edible

WHEN CRUSHED, THE LEAVES OF THIS PLANT emit an odor reminiscent of lemons. This odor may also resemble that of oregano, especially late in the season. Its purple flowers are highly attractive to butterflies, bees and hummingbirds. This pretty plant from the Monarda family often appears in large masses. Lemon Mint is very easy to grow and often forms large colonies. It can become aggressive if given optimum growing conditions. It is susceptible to powdery mildew. Be sure to plant in full sun and rich soil for best results.

Monarda citriodora's highly ornate flower structure looks very much like its perennial native cousin, *Monarda punctata.* Lemon Beebalm is a long-lived fresh-cut flower. I love the way it sometimes spikes and then gently curls over like a kitten's paw, giving movement to an arrangement.

Lion's Tail ❧ *Leonotis leonurus*
Wild Dagga

I STARTED GROWING LION'S TAIL YEARS ago because the entire plant and especially the structure of the orange flowers look so very bizarre. In South Africa, Lion's Tail is an evergreen shrub that grows up to six feet tall and four feet wide. In my garden, it's a lean, tall annual. Lion's Tail flowers look amazing in bouquets and will dry successfully right in the vase. The orange color and tubular shape of Lion's Tail offer clues about its co-evolution with African sunbirds, as their curved bills are well-suited for feeding from these flowers.

LION'S TAIL

Height: 3' - 8'

Color: Orange

Bloom Time: Mid-summer through fall

Light: Full sun

Soil: Loam or amended clay

Moisture: Dry to medium

Native to: South Africa

Annual

Not Everlasting

Not Edible

Mexican Sunflower ❧ *Tithonia rotundifolia*

MEXICAN SUNFLOWERS THRILL ME EACH summer with their mass production of blossoms. I enjoy deadheading these enthusiastic bloomers all summer long for an extra zap of orange energy in the garden. They bloom all season, right up to frost. Mexican Sunflowers last in bouquets three to six days.

MEXICAN SUNFLOWER

Height: 3' - 6'

Color: Vivid orange

Bloom time: Mid-summer through fall

Light: Full sun

Soil: Average to good

Moisture: Dry to medium

Native to: Southwestern United States extending into Central America

Annual

Not Everlasting

Not Edible

Snapdragon ❧ *Antirrhinum majus*
Dragon Flower

SNAPDRAGON

Height: 1.5' - 3.5'

Color: Mixed

Bloom Time: Mid-summer through fall

Light: Full Sun

Soil: Loam or amended clay

Moisture: Dry to medium

Native to: Rocky areas of Europe, the United States and North Africa

Annual

Not Everlasting

Not Edible

SNAPDRAGONS ARE A GOOD, OLD-FASHIONED, easy-to-grow cut flower that will re-bloom over and over again with deadheading! They begin blooming at the bottom of the stalk and work their way up. Their common names derive from the way the flowers look like opening mouths when pressed on their sides. The flowers are snapped shut and require more pressure to open than a honey bee can provide, so Snapdragons rely on heavier bumblebees for their pollination. I grow two varieties: the old-fashioned 'Rocket' and a new variety, 'Chantilly,' that features huge, open-faced, butterfly-shaped flowers that are lightly scented and longer-lived in the garden and vase than old-fashioned snapdragons. The Latin name, *Antirrhinum*, means "like a snout" and refers to the seed pod's resemblance to a calf's nose.

Strawflower *Helichrysum bracteatum*

STRAWFLOWER

Height: 1' - 2'

Color: Mixed

Bloom Time: Mid-summer through fall

Light: Full Sun

Soil: Loam or amended clay

Moisture: Dry to medium

Native to: Africa, Australasia and Eurasia

Annual

Everlasting

Not Edible

STRAWFLOWERS ARE AN OLD-FASHIONED favorite of mine! Another popular plant from the '80s era of everlastings, Strawflowers are very easy to grow. Their unusual, papery dry structure is a dead giveaway that they were designed for survival in hot, dry climates. They come in a variety of vivid or soft colors. Like many everlastings, proper timing to harvest for drying is key. If you want a perfectly-formed dried flower, the best time to harvest for drying is when the two outer layers of bracts are open. If you delay harvesting, you get an overblown, funky, bright yellow dried flower; it's as if Salvador Dalí and his aesthetic of melted clocks suddenly started growing and drying Strawflowers.

Sweet Annie ❦ *Artemisia annua*

Annual Wormwood, Sweet Sagewort, Sweet Wormwood

FOR YEARS I WALKED AMONG FORESTS OF Sweet Annie that I grew to use as filler in fresh and dried bouquets and as the base for everlasting wreaths. Sweet Annie has fern-like leaves, a distinctive sweet scent (thus its name!) and a great ability to self-sow. With a little encouragement, these annuals grow into Christmas tree-sized plants in one growing season! Sweet Annie plants can reach six to eight feet high and two to three feet wide. I recommend making Sweet Annie wreath bases from freshly harvested branches when the stems are still quite pliable.

SWEET ANNIE

Height: 2' - 8'

Color: Green

Bloom Time: Late summer and fall

Light: Full sun

Soil: Loam or amended clay

Moisture: Dry to medium

Native to: Eurasia

Annual

Everlasting

Not Edible

Tall Verbena ❦ *Verbena bonariensis*

Purpletop Vervain, Clustertop Vervain, Pretty Verbena, South American Vervain

TALL VERBENA

Height: 2' - 3'

Color: Purple

Bloom Time: Mid-summer through fall

Light: Full sun

Soil: Loam

Moisture: Dry to medium

Native to: South America

Annual

Not Everlasting

Not Edible

A BELOVED GARDEN DESIGN AND CUTTING garden flower, *Verbena bonariensis* is delightfully drought-tolerant and beloved by pollinators. Strangely, most people seem to know *Verbena bonariensis* best by its Latin name! In fact I've never run across any of the common names I have listed here! Because of its long, thin, tall stems and flat purple blossoms, *Verbena bonariensis* looks amazing in the garden, giving any area an intriguing see-through quality. If planted en masse, it shows as a powerful blast of purple. It can be used effectively as a background flower or, when massed, as a featured flower. Its only downside is its strong tendency to self-sow, which has raised concerns that it may become invasive in a number of areas.

Zinnia ❦ *Zinnia elegans* (Common) and *Z. haageana* (Mexican)

ZINNIA

Height: 2' - 4' *(Z. elegans)*; 1' - 2' *(Z. haageana)*

Color: Mixed

Bloom Time: Mid-summer through fall

Light: Full sun

Soil: Rich soil

Moisture: Dry to medium

Native to: Originated in dry grasslands of southwestern United States and down to South America; most varieties found in central Mexico

Annual

Not Everlasting

Not Edible

HANDS DOWN, ZINNIAS ARE PURE JOY! I HAVE yet to meet someone in the world who does not love the cheerful, colorful faces of zinnias. Every year I experiment with different varieties. I recommend growing a mixed bag of colors and varieties. Zinnias are in their glory in late summer and are one of the last annuals to succumb to the cold. They tend to be immune to early frosts, making their vivid hues all the more precious as summer slips away. Zinnias are a cut-and-come-again variety of flower, which means the more blossoms you cut, the more this flower grows and re-blooms. That means blossoms all season long – as close as an annual gets to being sustainable!

Zulu Daisy ❦ *Venedium fastuosum*

THIS FLOWER IS AN ABSOLUTE CONVERSATION starter in a garden or a fresh bouquet; Zulu Daisies have bright white petals that contrast dramatically with centers of hot orange and dark black. These exotic flowers bloom fast and furiously and require frequent deadheading to keep the show going through the entire summer, but they are well worth the effort!

ZULU DAISY

Height: 1' - 2'

Color: White with orange and black interior

Bloom Time: Early summer through late summer

Light: Full sun

Soil: Loam or amended clay

Moisture: Dry to medium

Native to: Africa

Annual

Not Everlasting

Not Edible

FIVE

Making Babies

Sowing seeds is like being a little kid again. You get to play with dirt and water! Were you one of those kids who collected shells, leaves or rocks? I was a collector of the unusual. I'd run my fingers over and around my treasures again and again as if they were Greek worry beads. Then I'd stow the magical item in my pocket as a good luck charm. Connecting with the beauty of nature always made me feel confident and safe.

* * *

Bringing Life into the World - From Babies to Seedlings

Before I fell in love with flowers, my life had been devoted to nurturing new life as a childbirth educator, midwife, and pre-natal and postpartum fitness instructor. I had developed a prenatal fitness program for the Los Angeles YMCA, then moved to Toronto where I began Preggae Woman, Canada's first pre-natal and postpartum fitness program. I guess that made me a natural for midwifing other beautiful life forms into this world.

It amazes me to realize I've been growing flowers for over a quarter of a century. I'm so excited to share my passion with you. Let's make beautiful flowers together!!

Getting Started

I can say with confidence that growing wildflowers from seed *is not difficult*. As with herbs and vegetables (and baking cookies), you just follow the step-by-step directions in the proper order and voila!

Choosing the proper growing medium is the most important part of successfully growing plants from seed.

First things first: growing medium. Providing your seeds with the right kind of growing medium is **the** most important thing you can do to help them succeed and thrive. Germination happens when seeds are provided with water, oxygen and a growing medium that allows roots to easily penetrate downward. Seedlings germinate and grow best in a fluffy, non-compacted growing medium, or soilless mix, that will stay moist but never get soggy. You can find ready-made seed starting mediums at your local garden center or hardware store. Please do not use potting soil or garden soil! Potting soil is heavy and holds too much water. Garden soil is also too dense and may harbor insects or diseases that would kill your fragile, newly-formed seedlings.

Successful Seeding with Annuals and Perennials

I'm going to give you instructions for growing two types of flowers: annuals and perennials. The basic instructions below apply for most annuals. After that, we'll look at starting perennials, those flowers whose seeds need the grittiness and freeze-thaw action of winter in order to break down their hard shell and activate germination. I'll show you how to germinate perennials in winter climates; and if you live in warm winter areas, I'll show how you can cleverly fool the seeds into thinking they've gone through a freeze-thaw winter.

Annuals: the basic sow and grow

If you are seeding into a container, you'll want to plant two, or at the most three, seeds per pot. If you are starting many seedlings in a flat to transplant into small pots before planting outside, you'll want to plant seeds fairly close together; but make sure the plants do not crowd each other. Plants are competing for light, water and nourishment, so when the seedlings have their first set of leaves, use a pair of tweezers to remove extraneous plants. Make your decision based on spacing rather than the quality of the seedling.

Drop the seeds individually onto the surface of the soil, pressing each down lightly to surround the seed with moisture. This moisture encourages the decomposition of the seed coat, facilitating germination. Most seeds need to be very lightly covered with growing medium and then pressed down with your hand so there is good seed-to-soil contact. Be sure not to bury the seeds too deeply. To germinate

A cotyledon is the first green shoot to poke through the soil. It contains a set of leaves different from those the plant will have for the rest of its life and its main purpose is to process sunlight.

The traditional rule of thumb for seeding is that with very fine seeds use no more than four seeds per square inch of surface. Larger seeds should be seeded at two seeds per square inch of surface.

properly, it's better to keep the seed very close to the surface of the soil than to bury it too deeply.

Seed package instructions will tell you if a species needs to be surface sown. This means the species requires light to grow. Carefully sow the seeds on top of the growing medium and then press down with your hand. Brush off your hands over the container to be sure no seeds are stuck to your hand.

Perennials: sowing their seeds in winter

Nature's way: when a wildflower seed drops to the ground in the fall, it will start out on the surface of the soil, being gently covered with falling leaves, petals and other natural debris; throughout the winter the weight of the snow presses the seed down into the soil. In the spring, as snow melts, the earth draws the seed further downward. As the soil warms up, the damp seed's hard shell will have deteriorated enough to allow the tiny cotyledon to germinate.

But what if we want to participate in the perennial seed germination process ourselves and not leave it all to Mother Nature? Enter *cold, moist stratification,* or *winter sowing*: the artificial reconstruction of winter conditions. Yes, you can actually fool wildflowers into thinking they have gone through winter.

Here are two methods, depending on your winter temperatures.

Method 1:
Wintering outside.

If you have cold, wintery conditions where you live, you can plant seeds in pots, place them outside and let nature do the work.

What you'll need: wildflower seed, pots with a drainage hole, growing medium, label, indelible marker

Directions

1. Fill pots with growing medium up to one inch (2.5 cm) below the brim.

2. Place three equally spaced seeds in each pot.

3. Cover the seeds with ⅛-inch (0.5 cm) of soil.

4. Gently press down so there is good seed-to-soil contact.

5. Label and date the pot(s) so you know what and when you have planted.

6. Be sure to use an indelible marker so you can read the label in spring.

7. Place the pots outside and wait at least six to eight weeks before bringing them inside to grow.

Letting your wildflower seeds experience true winter is the easiest way to break down the hard seed coat.

When a young seedling receives an unbalanced amount of light and nutrients, they can become long and thin, often resulting in weak plants. Your plants should not have to stretch to receive light.

Your Babies Are Growing!

As the plant grows bigger it will use food and water faster. The larger the plant the more it transpires, or sweats, and the more it drinks. The roots will begin to take up more and more room in the pot, leaving less room for soil. Since soil retains moisture, a pot crowded with roots will require watering more frequently. When it's hot and sunny, your plant will lose a great

A plant's set of first true leaves emerge quickly after the cotyledon in order to continue photosynthesis and plant growth.

If you have planted many seeds in a flat or large container, now is the time you will be moving each seedling to its own separate container. If you have planted several seeds in small pots, now is the time you will need to be sure only one seedling is growing in each small pot.

The purpose of transplanting is to give each seedling enough space, light, air and nutrition to grow to about six inches tall. Each seedling will be given approximately three square inches of soil that is at least four inches deep.

Over the next six weeks the roots of the plants will plunge deep into every corner of the container. Begin by watering deeply the flat or containers the seedlings are growing in.

During transplanting the roots of seedlings must stay moist. Separate the seedlings growing in flats by ever so carefully breaking up the soil in the flat. Slowly and gently coax apart the plants so that each

deal of water and may need to be watered twice a day. Water a drooping plant thoroughly to help it recover.

Movin' On Up – Transplanting Your Babies

When seeds germinate, they become seedlings. First, tiny cotyledons emerge and their roots go into the soil. Next, the first true set of leaves appear. Now is the time for the second stage in the seeding process – transplanting.

This is a delightful process: it's fascinating to observe a plant's leaf structure and the fragility of each root system.

Each pot must contain only one seedling to reduce competition for nutrients, water and light.

SIX

Get in the Garden!

I am a totally self-taught gardener. When I fell in love with flowers, I wanted to learn absolutely everything about them. I read every gardening book, website, catalogue, and magazine I could get my hands on. Whenever I traveled, I visited every garden center and public garden I possibly could. All the while, I was experimenting: combining different plants in the garden, seeing how large each plant became as it grew and learning by trial and error to find out exactly where each plant liked to live on my property.

Your gardening style will come to you

When you enter a garden or meadow, allow yourself to be entertained. Let it draw you in. You'll soon discover what thrills you, piques your interest, and what catches your eye. You are sure to find plants and combinations you think are really cool. Observe the way that standing or sitting in a certain spot in a garden makes you feel. These experiences are the treasure map to discovering your own garden design style.

Conehead joy

First...The Basics

There are three important things for you to understand about the site you have to work with:

1. Your soil type
2. The amount of sunlight it receives
3. The natural ebb and flow of moisture the area receives

Understanding your Soil

A major factor in determining how well your wildflower plants or seeds will grow is their compatibility with the soil in your garden. Each wildflower species has a range of soil types in which it will flourish. It is very important to choose plants that will thrive in your specific conditions.

Soil Types

Soils can be divided into three general classifications: sands, loams and clays. There is great variation within these broad groups, but these categories will suffice for the purpose of describing where a given plant will or will not grow.

- **Sandy Soils** are very easy to dig in, dry out very quickly and tend to have very little organic or nutrient-rich material.
- **Clay Soils** are challenging to dig in, tend to be a mucky mess in the spring and create a dry, crusty surface in the summer time. Clay soils remain moist under their crusty surface and are filled with wonderful minerals and nutrients that produce healthy plants.
- **Loamy Soils** offer the best of both worlds. Easy to dig in, loamy soils retain just the right amount of moisture and are a nutrient-rich environment for plants.

The Lump Test – The easiest way to figure out what kind of soil you have is to grab a shovel and dig. When you dig into clay soil, it will form hard clumps that refuse to fall apart. When you dig into loamy soil, any lumps you dig up will easily fall apart with a nudge from your shovel. Sandy soil will crumble easily.

Gardening in Break-Your-Shovel Clay or Pure Beach Sand?

Rejoice! There are many gorgeous wildflower species that thrive in extreme conditions. See page 190 for a detailed list of clay or sand-loving plants.

Shedding Light on Light

It helps to know what the light requirements mean when you read about a plant:

Full sun = 4-6 hours of sunshine
Part shade = 2-4 hours of sunshine
Dappled shade = consistent indirect light
Deep shade = 1-2 hours of sunshine or less

Amending – Is it Worth the Time, Effort and Expense?

It's likely that you will have a love-at-first-sight moment at the garden center. Then when you finally read the plant tag you discover it will not grow in your conditions. So you proceed to drastically alter your conditions to suit the needs of that plant. Be advised: amending your soil to suit the needs of plants is an expensive, time-consuming and largely futile process. A patch of earth will always return to its original conditions unless you are prepared for the ongoing effort and expense it takes to amend those conditions every year. Save your compost for growing your vegetables and annual flowers!

One of the marvelous things about wildflowers is that they are utterly self-sufficient. They have thrived on the planet for literally ages – without any human intervention. Once your wildflower garden is established, no watering, fertilizing or deadheading is necessary. If you are transplanting a wildflower into the garden, you will need to water it generously over a period of six to eight weeks while it becomes established. After that, all you need to do is cut down the spent stems every spring.

I spend about one hour a year maintaining my wildflower gardens. Twenty minutes or so is spent cutting down the dead stems and about forty minutes divided up over the entire season for occasional weeding. If allowed in your municipality or region, you may wish to add another twenty minutes of maintenance to burn the spent stems and then distribute their nutritious ashes throughout the garden. Please remember that your wildflower garden or meadow is a supermarket and ingenious housing complex for beneficial wildlife. Be sure to leave the seed heads and foliage standing all winter for them to eat! I find their scrawny shapes oddly comforting. They remind me that winter will not last forever and soon the wildflowers will return.

Coreopsis time

Meadow 101:
Ecosystem Gardening

Whether you are planting a wildflower garden from transplants or sowing a wildflower meadow from seed, understanding how meadows function is important. A wildflower meadow is a natural, living ecosystem that combines wildflowers and native grasses. In traditional European-style high-maintenance gardening, plants are two or more feet apart and thus require ongoing mulching, weeding, watering and fertilizing. In a meadow or meadow-style garden, plants are positioned one plant per square foot or closer.

The underground world of wildflowers and native grasses.

A meadow-style garden needs no mulching or watering. When you plant wildflowers close together, as nature does, the plants provide their own shade and water conservation, and you leave less room for weeds to invade the space. You get even more low-maintenance benefits when you include native grasses in your wildflower garden: the wide, fibrous roots of the grasses mesh with the deep, vertical roots of the flowers, creating an impenetrable barrier that eliminates most weedy invaders.

This tight-knit plant community will thrive for many years with minimum maintenance. Want proof? Plan a visit to the oldest man-made meadow grown from seed: the Curtis Prairie. Located at the University of Wisconsin Arboretum in Madison, Wisconsin, The Curtis Prairie was planted in 1934 and is still going strong.

Gardens and meadows evolve. Weather conditions change from year to year favoring certain species. One year, the conditions might be perfect for Yellow Coneflowers *(Ratibida pinnata)*; another year might offer optimum conditions for Meadow Blazingstars *(Liatris ligulistylis)*. Over time, gardens and meadows evolve into pleasing swaths of color, pattern and texture.

Editing your garden. I love to recruit volunteers into my gardens! Volunteers are plants that occur naturally or self-sow on their own, rather than being deliberately planted by you. Once you begin to recognize certain seedlings, you can choose to enhance sections of your garden by leaving the seedlings where they are growing, editing some out or moving a few to different parts of the garden.

Editing my gardens is an ongoing and highly personal form of self-expression. Sometimes I'm experimenting with color; sometimes it's texture or height. Warning! – with certain wildflowers, like Blue False Indigos or Purple Prairie Clovers, you have only one year to decide where they will live in the garden because they will form taproots ten feet or deeper. Luckily, a good number of wildflowers have shallow roots and can be moved around. The goal of a successful transplanting project is to shovel so wide and deep around the plant it has no idea you moved it! Most importantly, observe from season to season where your wildflowers are thriving. They will demonstrate to you where they are happiest!

I appreciate the way naturalistic garden designer Duncan Brine takes his cues from nature. In a wide-ranging conversation with him, he touched on subjects close to my heart: "Collaborate with nature," he advised. "Learn from reseeders the art of judicious editing. The plants will show you where they want to be. Traditional gardens are static; naturalistic gardens have growth and change built into them. They are designed for growth because nature is constantly changing."

A Meadow-Inspired Pollinator Garden

Dimensions: 8' x 15'

Flowers and Grasses in the Pollinator Garden: Beebalm, Black-Eyed Susan, Blanketflower, Blue Flax, Coreopsis, Cup Plant, Ironweed, Little Bluestem, Meadow Blazingstar, Pale Purple Coneflower, Prairie Blazingstar, Prairie Dropseed, Purple Coneflower, Purple Prairie Clover, 'Silver King' Artemisia, Sky Blue Aster

Maintenance: Ultra-minimal! I weed my Pollinator Garden for a total of one hour a year, if that. And I never, ever water or fertilize!

This Wildflower Pollinator Garden is a great example of a fantasy wildflower meadow. Its random placement of flowers and grasses mimics a meadow but does not copy it exactly. In nature, a meadow is

Meadow magic in August; Ox-Eye Sunflowers; Black Eyed Susans, Prairie Blazingstar and Rattlesnake Master

composed of 75-80% wildflowers and 25-30% native grasses. My Pollinator Garden is 90% wildflowers and 10% native grasses.

Note: The principles of meadow ecology work for informal and formal style gardens. Just be sure to plant wildflowers and grasses at a distance of one plant per square foot.

Marielle Anzelone: An Urban Wildflower Gardener

Marielle Anzelone, who lives in an apartment in New York City with her husband and children, has no personal gardening space. She is the founder of Wildflower Week in NYC – a year-round program that nurtures New Yorkers' inner naturalists.

A passionate advocate for urban wildflowers, Marielle has designed and built native gardens

Columbines grow in Marielle Anzelone's 2400 sq. ft. native plant garden in Union Square, Manhattan

throughout the city. "Native plants help define our cities and create a unique sense of place. They are critical to urban biodiversity and habitats for wildlife. We humans can't continue to fill our landscapes with plants just for our aesthetic pleasure. Nearly all North American birds feed their nestlings insects only.

Wildflowers in Manhattan! Marielle Anzelone created this 2400 sq. foot native plant garden in Union Square in the heart of Manhattan

If we want birds, we need bugs. And if we want those bugs, including the caterpillars that turn into butterflies, we need native plants."

My first meadow – the dream and the reality

When we moved to the country, I knew I wanted a meadow to be my special place; my creative and spiritual home. I dove straight into buying a large can of seeds that said "Northeastern Wildflower Meadow Mix." We were rural newbies (or, as I later learned the proper term, "citiots"). My husband borrowed a bright orange tractor from some dear neighbors and tilled the half-acre of land several times until it seemed like every weed was gone and our patch of

soil was ready. Right before my eyes, my dream was coming true!

Here is a list of the mostly non-native flower seeds that were in the bag:

> Annual Poppies, Baby Blue Eyes, Baby's Breath, Black-Eyed Susan, Blanketflower, Blue Flax, Calendula, Candytuft, Coreopsis, Cornflowers, Cosmos, Echinacea, Gloriosa Daisy, Love-in-a-Mist, Maltese Cross, Pink Yarrow, Purple Dame's Rocket, Red Flax, Shasta Daisies, Sweet William, various wallflowers and White Yarrow.

I longed for the serenity a wildflower meadow brings; Yellow Coneflower, Prairie Blazingstar, Rattlesnake Master.

Several weeks went by. Each day I inspected my meadow, searching for signs of life. I was proud of myself when I recognized the feathery leaves of the White and Pink Yarrow. I was even more impressed when I recognized both the Shasta Daisy and the Maltese Cross leaves. Soon, a few blue Cornflowers appeared, as well as some brightly colored Red Poppies. But I also noticed there were leaves all over of a plant I had trouble identifying.

A good old-fashioned plant identification book (no Internet in those days!) told us we had Canada Thistle in our meadow. Yikes! I thought that tilling the land would have banished all weeds. Turns out tilling Canada Thistle breaks the roots into little bits, and

Canada Thistle is an alien plant notoriously difficult to banish from the garden.

each bit happily takes hold to make more and more plants. No way could we weed them all out! So, we let the meadow be and waited to see what else would emerge.

That first year, our meadow produced some lovely, non-native annual blue Cornflowers, the occasional Red Poppy, Pink Yarrow and purple Dame's Rocket. The perennial flowers, we knew, would not bloom until their second year. We were hopeful that our meadow would truly become a thing of beauty.

Year two arrived, and we were excited to see non-native red Maltese Crosses and white Shasta Daisies, in addition to the non-native purple Dame's Rocket and Pink Yarrow. No blue Cornflowers or Red Poppies, though. Some pretty little non-native yellow wallflowers, a biennial (blooms in the second year then dies). And some pretty, but prickly, purple Canada Thistles as well.

Year three included Shasta Daisies, Maltese Crosses and a veritable ocean of Canada Thistles.

Year four... we ripped it all out and started again.

What happened here? Turns out we did pretty much everything wrong, starting with choosing the wrong seed mix...

The Right Kind of Seed for the Location and Good Site Preparation
A meadow mix with a name that corresponds to your region is rarely one that will succeed. Why? Because the conditions within every region vary enormously and most of the species will not be native. Your neighbor may have clay soil, and you, sandy soil. Even within the boundaries of your own property, dramatic variations in sun, soil and moisture likely

exist. A genuine wildflower meadow mix – the kind you want – pays close attention to the type of soil, the amount of sunlight and moisture the area naturally receives.

Proper organic site preparation includes killing off super-aggressive weeds (like the Canada Thistles) with systematic and repeated tillings over a one-to-two-year period of time. Tilling Canada Thistles

How wonderful, I imagined, to joyfully gather wildflower bouquets with my daughter

just once or twice simply spreads their roots around and creates more plants! I still wanted a meadow. Surely, if this was the wrong way to grow a meadow, there must be a right way. Indeed there is, and we now have a beautiful two-acre meadow here at Wildflower Farm. It is filled with Beebalm, Big Bluestem, Butterflyweed, Coreopsis, Hoary Vervain, Indiangrass, Little Bluestem, Pale Purple Coneflower, Purple Coneflower, Purple Prairie Clover, Side Oats Grama, Spiderwort and Wild Quinine.

My Edible Herbal Wildflower Garden

My edible herbal wildflower garden here at the farm is an example of the design style I like to call "Painting with Plants." I love planting giant swaths of undulating color that add contrast between short carpets of textured plants, towered over by humongous, tall plants. The plants interact with one another, dancing in many directions all at once. This garden combines annual herbs, flowers and vegetables with perennial herbs, heirloom flowers and wildflowers. It's a jumble and swirl garden and I love it!

Here's the list of every single plant packed into this ten-foot-square garden.

Note: I've listed plants by category, but many plants fit in several.

Herbs
Anise Hyssop (native plant), Bronze Fennel, Creeping Thyme, Dill, Genovese Basil, Lion's Tail, Mountain Mint (native plant), 'Purple Ruffles' Basil, Sage, Thai Basil, Variegated Sage, Wild Rose

Edible Flowers
Borage, Cardoon, Lavender, Marigold, Nasturtium, Pansies, Scarlet Runner Bean, Spiderwort

Fruits
Alpine Strawberries, Native Strawberries

Heirloom Flowers
Black-Eyed Susan (vine), *Celosia*, Hollyhock, Hops, *Verbascum* (Mullein), Zinnia

Veggies
Purple Kale, Spinach

Wildflowers
Monarda, Mountain Mint, Nodding Wild Onion, Pale Purple Coneflower, Rattlesnake Master, Wild Quinine

Lavender hyssop, Celosia and the Scarlet Runner Bean vine dance the tango

Maintenance: This tiny garden needs about 20 minutes of weeding a week, a little regular watering, and runs on the built-in fertilizing engine we call compost.

Composting Basics

By integrating organic material (compost) into our gardens, we are continuing a several-thousand-year-old tradition carried out by many ancient civilizations. If you're thinking to yourself that you don't produce enough to warrant a composter, think again! About 35% of what you put in the garbage can be redirected to a composter. It is wise to build or buy some sort of holding container for your scraps to keep it together and to keep out curious wildlife (including the neighbor's cat). Store your compost bin somewhere convenient and close enough to the door to cut down on excuses not to make regular visits.

So, what goes in? Simple: if it came from the earth, it can go back to the earth. Avoid bones, meat, and anything fatty, as these will only serve to attract rodents and other hungry animals. Yard and kitchen scraps (but nothing woody), garden cuttings and grass clippings will break down well and become compost.

It will take a little while to build up enough bulk material to be useful in your gardens, and it will take a little time to break down, too. Be patient. As for turning your compost – introducing air into the pile periodically – the jury's still out. Do it if you want, but there's no real obligation.

Eco-Lawns and Compost

The easiest path to a healthy, organic lawn is to top-dress with compost every fall. Anytime you are over-seeding or seeding a new lawn, use compost as a gentle, natural, slow-release fertilizer. I happen to know a lot about lawns because Paul and I developed a wonderfully low maintenance, drought-tolerant

Raised bed built with compost and planted with seedlings

in shaded areas where the compacted clay needs drastic amendment. I build the beds 1½ -2 feet deep in compost. The woodland wildflowers love it as they thrive naturally in the ancient forests floors filled with humus and decaying trees, bark and moss – rich, organic material that is very much like the compost you make yourself.

My Shoemaker's Children's Gardens

In my backyard, hidden from public view, are my private gardens. From my perch at the kitchen sink, I can gaze out into the full sun garden framed by our lush, green lawn of fine fescue grasses. My tiny, hidden shade garden hugs the back wall of the house. I call these two gardens my Shoemaker's Children's Gardens because they receive so little

combination of native grasses that we call Eco-Lawn. This lawn grows beautifully in full sun, part shade, deep shade and even under pine trees. It's quick to germinate but slow to grow, so our native grass mix needs mowing just once a month, or just a few times a year for a more relaxed lawn look. You'll find more information about Eco-Lawn in the digital Resource Guide of www.tamingwildflowers.com.

Natural Raised Bed
You can stuff a whole lot of plants into a small bed with our now not-so-secret ingredient: compost.

I love building natural-looking raised beds with compost. I began using this technique on my pick-your-own flower farm many years ago. Each spring, I sculpted raised beds for my annuals, creating undulating shapes around my perennial beds. I also use compost to build natural-looking raised beds

A favorite combination for late spring; Giant Alliums, Blanketflowers and Chives

Wild Quinine lights up my shade garden

attention. They are stuffed to the gills with colors, textures and shapes of all sizes; not all of the plants are natives. I am constantly experimenting with which plants will succeed in the temperamental full sun garden on the edge of our septic system and gleefully discovering extra space for plants in my tiny pocket of a shade garden.

Plants for my full sun garden:
Big Bluestem, Blue False Indigo, Butterflyweed, Butterfly Bush, Creeping Thyme, Crocosmia, Crocus, Culver's Root, Fall Crocus or Colchicum, Giant Allium, Giant Imperial Fritillaria, Great Blue Lobelia, Helianthus maximilliani, Hydrangea, Indiangrass, Joe-Pye Weed, Native Columbine, Nodding Wild Onion, Orange Iris, Rattlesnake Master, Russian Sage, Showy Goldenrod, Smooth Penstemon, Speedwell, Tulip, Virginia Wild Rye, White False Indigo, and Wild Senna.

Plants in my shade garden:
Allium, Astrantia, Climbing Hydrangea, daylilies, Grecian Foxglove, Joe-Pye Weed, Lady's Mantle, Lysimachia, Meadow Rue, Persicaria, Pink Shooting Star, Turtlehead, Violets, and Wild Quinine. I have also recently added: Blue Flag Iris, Blue Vervain, Culver's Root, Meadow Blazingstar, New York Ironweed, and Red Milkweed.

My Sweet Scree Garden

A few years ago, Paul and I built a scree garden for wildflowers that thrive in poor soil, sand and gravel. The word scree is from the old Scottish word skridan, defined in the Merriam-Webster dictionary as "an accumulation of loose stones or rocky debris lying on a slope, or at the base of a hill or cliff." In other words, a scree garden is just a rock garden on a slope. A mixture of garden soil, sand and gravel is all that is required. My scree is on a flat expanse between my wildflower meadow and my gardens. You could also build a scree garden in a ditch, around a water feature or deck, or as a transition area from garden to woods.

Prairie Smoke and Blue Flax in the Springtime Scree Garden

How to build your own wildflower scree garden

Dig a one-foot ditch in a very sunny spot in an open area with great air circulation. Placing stepping stones around the area will be useful as you construct the garden. Begin with a layer of gravel,

Paul moves big rocks to form scree hill

The scree is made from rocks and various grades of gravel; Now it's time to add the soil.

broken stones and bricks in varying heights to create a natural effect. The next layer consists of half crushed stone or gravel, a quarter sand or grit and a quarter soil. Water the entire area to compress the materials and avoid air pockets.

On page 190 you will find a list of wildflowers you can grow that thrive in rock and scree garden conditions.

Cascading wine cups form deep roots in the hot, sunny scree garden.

The Non-Native Cutting Garden
(my dirty little addiction)

I have been growing cutting garden annuals and perennials for over 25 years. My hardy, perennial wildflower cutting gardens are the very definition of low maintenance; they grow beautifully without watering, mulching, fertilizing or deadheading. My annual cutting gardens are quite the opposite! Like vegetable gardens, annuals require uber-nutritious soil, loads of watering and constant vigilance to ward off insects and diseases. But the reward for all that hard work is well worth it. The visual sucker punch of annuals never fails to knock me off my feet. This year's cheap thrills included:

Low growing beauties for borders:
(short-stemmed but highly useful in small arrangements)
Anchusa, California native annuals: Tidy Tips, Hayfield Tarweed, Mountain Garland; 'Empress of India' Nasturtium, Farewell to Spring, *Cerinthe*, *Coleus* Creeping *Zinnia*, *Sanvitalia* 'Giant Exhibition', Dusty Miller, *Gazania* Globe Amaranth: 'Strawberry Fields' and Formula Mix (everlasting); Mammoth Pansy, 'Riveria' Blue Lobelia, Safari Marigold (everlasting).

Medium Height Beauties
Borage, Dill, Fennel, Perilla or Shiso; 'Aton', 'Genovese' and 'Siam Queen' Basils; Rainbow Swiss Chard, 'Redbor' Kale, *Amaranthus* 'Red Tails' and 'Green Tails' (everlasting), Celosia: 'Sunday

Orange', 'Pampas Plume' and Cristata Mix (everlasting); Craspedia (everlasting), *Dahlia* mixed, *Delphinium* (everlasting), Euphorbia 'Snow on the Mountain', *Gossypium* (Cotton) (everlasting), Helichrysum: 'Swiss Giants Mix' (everlasting), *Larkspur* 'QIS Carmine' and 'Dark Blue' (everlasting), Lilies, *Monarda Citriodora*, Salvia 'Red Jewel' and 'Victoria', Snapdragons: 'Chantilly' and 'Rocket Mix'; Statice: QIS Formula Mixture and 'Sunset' (everlasting), *Venidium* 'Zulu Prince', Verbena bonariensis, Zinnia: 'Pink Senorita', 'Aztec Sunset', Giant Flowered Mix, 'Benary's Giant'.

Towering Beauties
Cosmos, Kiss-Me-Over-the-Garden-Gate (everlasting), Lion's Tail, Morning Glory 'Grandpa Ott', Scarlet Runner Bean, Sunflowers – mixed, *Tithonia rotundifolia*

The Cycle of Beauty
Each spring I am compelled to witness green-leaved babies burst forth from the ground. I nurture their fragile lives into strong and beautiful participants in the collaboration between pollinators and pure beauty. Flowers then coerce me to celebrate their splendor in floral arrangements large and small. In the next chapter I'll show you simple techniques and flower combinations that will enable you to confidently create stunning floral designs all season long. Your heart will be soaring in no time!!! 🌷

Glowing orange zinnia floats above the annual cutting garden in summertime.

SEVEN

Your Wildflower Design Studio

Wildflowers signify the emotional connection between the earth and nature, a celebration of life, optimism and overcoming adversity. What subconscious message do you convey when you create a wildflower bouquet? It's the very opposite of grabbing a random bouquet of flowers likely imported from a large commercial operation in South America, where flowers are forced into bloom with petroleum-based fertilizers and workers and flowers alike are exposed to harmful pesticides. No, this is wildflower gardening: free from pesticides and fertilizers; a practice overflowing with unbridled beneficent beauty.

* * *

Picking wildflowers is an intimate collaboration with nature where you are "in the moment," truly seeing and celebrating a bounty of colors, shapes and textures. Designing with wildflowers is a spontaneous act that demonstrates a gentle sense of adventure and a deep respect for the landscape.

For many years, Paul and I produced elaborate outdoor weddings at our wildflower farm. For one of these weddings, a most lavish affair, the bride had always dreamed of including cream-colored hydrangeas in her bridal bouquet. Well, I grew hundreds of kinds of flowers, but not hydrangeas! To make sure she had her dream flower, I journeyed to the wholesaler and purchased several to include in her bouquet.

Designing with wildflowers is just like designing with any flower. Be as creative as you want. Every design is different and you can never go wrong.

The morning of the wedding, I made a painful discovery about commercially grown flowers. Unbeknownst to me, the hydrangeas I had purchased were coated in harsh pesticides and preservatives that caused my eyes to turn red and sting like crazy. I wept through the entire wedding – not from joy, but because my eyes were working hard to expel the chemicals burning them. That's when I learned firsthand that chemical pesticides and preservatives are used on many commercially grown flowers – and that many florists actually work in latex gloves to protect their skin.

I like to use deep buckets with handles to make it easier to carry long-stemmed flowers.

That's not the type of creative bouquet design I want for you, so let's get down to the happy, chemical-free business of this chapter: harvesting your wildflower bounty, setting up your design space (either inside or outdoors), and creating heavenly bouquets and arrangements.

Harvesting

Now that you've grown your beautiful wildflower garden, you have a wealth of flowers at your disposal. Your design studio is where you can create gorgeous displays and bouquets, and for that I'll get you set up further along in the chapter. But first, you must harvest the flowers. This all comes down to what to pick, how best to pick them, and how to ensure they live as long and happily as possible. A few simple tips and tricks will help you through your wildflower harvest and get your beautiful bounty safely back to your design studio.

Harvesting Supplies
For picking flowers: kitchen scissors, clippers, three buckets of varying sizes (8" deep, 1' deep, 2' deep or 20, 30 and 60 cm) – handles are advisable.

Bucket and Water Management
Fill each bucket about three inches (eight centimeters) deep with water. You can vary the water amount, but make sure the buckets are manageable and functional. Fill them too full and the buckets will be way too heavy to carry around; fill them too little and your plants won't get enough water.

Container Hygiene

Bacteria can reduce the life of your cut flowers, but you can prevent a bacterial invasion with simple bucket and vase maintenance. Scrub the inside and outside of your containers with an anti-bacterial cleaner. There are three options: a solution of one part chlorine bleach to ten parts of water, any household disinfectant sanitizing spray cleaner, or any anti-bacterial wipes. Let the cleaning solution sit for at least four to five minutes before rinsing. Make sure buckets and vases are dry before stacking.

Honor Your Inner Wildflower Florist

Before you begin cutting: Slow down. Breathe. Leave your buckets and clippers behind and simply walk through the entire garden in a calm and observant manner. Take in the beauty. Notice the colors, shapes and textures that present themselves to you. Slow down further and allow yourself to notice less flashy flowers and foliage, perhaps an appealing pod or seed head. In that relaxed state, now head back to your bucket and clippers. Let's begin.

When You're Ready...

Using sharp scissors or gardening shears, cut as long a stem as possible. You can always make a stem shorter, but you can't lengthen it once it has been cut! Cut each stem at about a 45° angle. This increases exposed surface area, allowing the stem to absorb the most water. Before you place the stem in the water, strip off all the leaves and extraneous stems ¾ of the way to the top before

Remove leaves to reduce bacterial growth in the vase and cut your stems on an angle to increase water uptake.

you put it in the bucket. This will make for easier arranging later and reduce the amount of bacteria exposure to the stems.

Organize as you go. Keep like with like, and make sure all similar flowers are kept together. You'll sort them into further categories when you get to the design studio, but for now, placing similar flowers together will keep things simple.

When to Harvest

Always harvest at the coolest times of the day: early in the morning or in the evening. I do not recommend harvesting mid-day at the height of heat, as this is when flowers are most stressed. Morning harvesting between 7:30 and 9:30 is ideal. Plan to finish picking by 10 at the latest. If you are picking flowers on an exceptionally hot morning, find a shady spot nearby and leave the buckets there; then, after cutting and stripping the stems, quickly return to the bucket in the shade and plunge the stems into the cool water. Protect your newly cut flowers from the stress of the sun! If you are picking flowers in the evening, simply wait until the temperatures are noticeably cooler.

It's always best to gather your flowers in the morning and keep your buckets in the shade.

Thinking about Design Elements as You Pick

What to Pick

Every garden is filled with a variety of shapes, colors and textures. Choose what appeals to you. As you're harvesting, find flowers, foliage and pods whose color, texture and shape "speak" to you. Before long, you'll be capturing the wildness and naturalness of a meadow in a vase or container. Or, you may decide to create a very formal design. It's completely your choice! I've provided a list of design elements to keep in mind while harvesting from your wildflower garden. You're sure to enjoy experimenting with each of these. Primary elements will make your arrangement shine. Remember to include some background materials to make your bouquets look full, balanced and pleasing to the eye. The most important thing, however, is to pick the flowers that appeal to you.

Bouquets and arrangements can have multiple primary elements. In this design the Blue False Indigo and non-native Oriental Poppy are the primary elements that are complemented by the Mayapple leaf filler

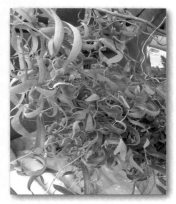

Curly Willow branches (pictured here) and Compass Plant leaves make excellent fillers in arrangements but also add interest with varying textures, shapes and movement.

Primary Elements: anything that catches your eye. It could be a spire or a daisy-shaped flower. Primary elements are the stars of an arrangement.
Background or Fill: material used to create a full appearance, add a curtain or backdrop to arrangements, or add texture without over-loading the bouquet with busy colors.

Understanding Your Shape Options

The floral world has provided us with more than just round, daisy-shaped flowers! There is a smorgasbord of shapes and textures available to add depth and interest to any bouquet.

SPIRES OR SPIKES

Spikes and spires, like the Hoary Vervain here, add variable height to an arrangement with rigid flower stalks that can be manipulated to the height you desire.

DAISY OR CIRCLE SHAPES

Circle-shaped flowers, like the Gaillardia and Black-Eyed Susan pictured here, are popular additions to an arrangement and are often used as primary elements.

BUTTONS AND GLOBES

Buttons and globes can be made up of one flower like Rattlesnake Master (pictured here) or multiple flowers that form a spherical shape like Red Milkweed.

PLUMES

Plumes are often found in grasses like this Indiangrass. They add texture and movement to an arrangement.

163

UMBEL AND FLAT TOPS
(An umbel is a group of short, umbrella-shaped flower stalks emanating outward from a central point)

Umbels or flat topped flowers, like the White Yarrow pictured here, are used as the base of many wedding bouquets but they can also add a swatch of color to an arrangement.

ENERGY AND MOVEMENT

Energy and movement come from anything that has a varying shape, like the Prairie Smoke here. They add interest, asymmetry, and a sense of wildness to an arrangement.

SOFT COLORS

Many wildflowers like Wild Quinine, Culver's Root, White Yarrow, *Monarda*, and Hoary Vervain, are soft colors that complement one another in an arrangement.

FUNKY BRANCHES, SEED HEADS AND PODS

Seed pods add so much texture to an arrangement and are often everlasting. Pictured here is Lavender Hyssop, Black Cohosh, Purple Coneflower, and Branched Coneflower.

SCREENS, CURTAINS AND FANS

Curtains and fans are used as a backdrop in arrangements. Native grasses, like the Little Bluestem pictured here, work well for this because they are tall and their colors do not overshadow the primary elements.

HOT COLORS

For a brightly-colored display, mix and match various colors like the bright yellows of Black-Eyed Susans, and Compass Plants with the reds found in Blanketflower and purples in the New England Aster and Rough Blazingstar.

EARTHY COLORS

Fall designs are often filled with the earthy tones of seed pods and heads and grasses gone to seed. Earthy tones can also be incorporated into colorful arrangements like the Little Blue Stem mixed with various yellows.

Setting Up Your Design Space

You've collected an assortment of wildflowers and now is the time to make yourself a design space where you can feel relaxed and creative. The best floral design spaces have large tables and good natural light. Working outside can also be enjoyable: just make sure you're in the shade to protect your floral harvest from the sun. Your design space doesn't have to be fancy - it just has to work for you. Once you're set up, the fun can begin!

Design Supplies

For arranging flowers: kitchen scissors, clippers, floral tape, floral picks, wire, frogs, fresh flower foam, dried flower foam, sand, gravel, glass stones and lots of vases of varying sizes and depths for displaying your flowers.

Container options. Almost anything can make an interesting container for an arrangement: mason

A vase can be anything from the traditional to the extreme. Let the flowers tell you which to choose…or try letting the vase tell you which flowers to pick.

jars, tea pots, tea cups, coffee pots and mugs, giant beverage coolers, antique bottles, watering cans, antique tins and unique or traditional vases. The world is filled with repurposing opportunities! Thrift stores, garage sales and overlooked treasures in your very own home are waiting to be rediscovered!

Prepare to Play

Step One: Re-sort, Refresh and Re-strip
When you first return from harvesting, fill five or six containers with cool water (use the cold water tap if you're drawing water from inside). Next, sort all the flowers you picked into design element categories: spires, circles, flat tops and umbels, background materials, pods. The goal is to make your designing process as easy as possible. As you sort the flowers recut each stem at an angle so it can take in water easily. To prevent bacteria from forming, make sure every stem is smooth to the touch and free of foliage

Having these items on hand will make your designing experience that much easier. Vase, various stones, scissors, foam, twine, floral tape, glue gun, picks, floral wire, and various frogs.

before you place it back in the water. Then place your well-organized containers filled with flowers in a semi-circle in front of you on your large work table.

Step Two: Relax and Enjoy!
Every spring, after a weather-enforced break from fresh floral design, I feel incredibly insecure handling fresh flowers again. By my second or third bouquet my chops are back and the fun begins. So, give yourself permission to just relax and play with flowers! Throw on some soothing (or energizing!) music to get the creative juices flowing. Don't be afraid to make mistakes! Mistakes are an essential part of the creative process. Feel free to tear any project apart. Enjoy a cup of tea then dive back into the creative flow.

Step Three: Choose a Container
If you haven't already chosen a vase or container, go ahead and choose one now. Think about where it will be displayed. Will it be seen only from the front and two sides or will your design be seen from all sides?

Flower Food for the Water
It's important to feed your flowers with sugar and help them fight off bacteria. There are many DIY flower food recipes available, but here's the one I tend to use: two tablespoons of lemon juice, one tablespoon of sugar and a quarter teaspoon of bleach in a quart (or one liter) of warm water. Expand the recipe as required. In an ideal universe the water should be changed each day. If you have time to

do that, great! If your life is as hectic as mine – you might miss a day or two. No cause for panic. Simply change the water and include new batch of flower food when you have the time.

Bouquet Design Basics

Build the framework
A frame of flowers will create a shape for the bouquet and hold the primary design flowers in place. Without it, your bouquet is likely to bunch to one side or fall apart. Build your frame with one or a number of background materials, so your primary elements will stand out. Use the photos below as guides or design your own framework.

Simple Stability. The stability for a simple arrangement comes from leaning the stems against the sides of the container. This style works well with narrow and deep containers.

More advanced stability. You can add weight to support a wide or shallow arrangement from below

Lean stems against the container for a relaxed look. Using a tall, clear vase is a great way to showcase the crisscrossing effect.

by placing sand, gravel, pebbles, foam or a heavy metal frog in the bottom of the container. This technique gives you the ability to place a stem at any angle you wish, and it will remain stable without having to lean against the sides of the container or against other stems.

Frogs are a simple way to stabilize the stems in an arrangement without having them lean against each other or the container. There are many types of frogs so choose the one that works best for you.

Adding Primary Design Elements

After your frame is built, it's time to add primary design elements. Make sure to arrange them in a way that shows off their beauty while still comple-menting the whole arrangement. This part of the design is all about your personal taste, so experi-ment freely. Here are a few tips for making a natural, balanced design, but remember that nothing is set in stone.

- Always work in odd numbers; it looks more natural.
- To achieve a relaxed but symmetrical-looking distribution of a primary design element, stroll around the arrangement to experience it from all angles.

- As you insert primary design elements, think about how to display its best qualities. For example, daisy-shaped flowers have a beautiful, forward-facing head. So make sure each daisy-shaped flower faces outward.

How to bunch flowers

A great technique to add swaths of color or depth is "bunching." Bunching is a flexible technique that can be used for secondary flowers or even your primary design element. You can bunch flowers to create a dense background or solid surface in your bouquet, or to show off groups of your primary element.

To bunch flowers you can use floral picks or floral tape. Picks help to stabilize thinner stems and make it easier to add to a floral foam brick.

Don't be afraid to make mistakes when designing an arrangement. Remember that nothing is permanent and if you want to make changes, go ahead! Experiment with colors, textures and shapes; with vases, techniques and designs.

DIY Everlastings

Dried bunches of everlasting flowers look gorgeous as décor enhancement.

You can use them in bouquets or in DIY projects such as the homemade wreath I describe below. The best part is that these beautiful arrangements are low maintenance and very long lasting. Couldn't be simpler! Here's how:

How to Dry Everlasting Flowers

There are two ways to dry flowers. You can harvest them fresh, band them with a rubber band, then hang them upside down in a dark room (or one with indirect light) with decent ventilation. Or, you can place the flowers in a vase with water and just not replenish the water. Keep the arrangement in indirect light. The flowers will dry upright and, depending upon the species, will last up to a year. If you don't want your everlastings to shed, once they are thoroughly dry you can spray them lightly with a cheap, lacquer-filled hairspray.

Easy DIY Everlasting Wreath

Background Materials

There are so many background materials for wreaths that work well! My favorite native ones are gold-enrod, Wild Yarrow and any kind of artemisia (I prefer either Sweet Annie, the annual artemisia, or Silver King, a perennial native).

The Building Process

1. Strip small branches into uniform lengths and combine at one end. Spread the unbound ends to make small fans. Bind the stems with floral tape.
2. You can either buy a wreath base at a craft store or you can braid floral wire to create an inexpensive one.

Strip small branches into uniform lengths and combine at one end. Spread the unbound ends to make small fans. Bind the stems with floral tape.

You can either buy a wreath base at a craft store or you can braid floral wire to create an inexpensive one.

Then wire the fans one on top of another all the way around the wreath base, making sure to cover the stems and tape from the previous fan.

3. Then wire the fans one on top of another all the way around the wreath base, making sure to cover the stems and tape from the previous fan.
4. Glue-gun dried flowers of your choice throughout the wreath. Voila!

If you've enjoyed following me through these design processes, I hope you have also been inspired to make your own ever-more-beautiful creations as you begin (or continue) to grow wild-flowers yourself! The benefits of growing wildflowers are endless, but surely one of the most rewarding is our ability to fashion freshly harvested wildflower bouquets! Having an array of natural, pesticide-free flowers at your fingertips is so rewarding. The tips and tricks to harvest and design floral bouquets I share here are intended to spark an innate ability that resides in you to produce your own wildly beautiful floral masterpieces. 🦌

EIGHT

The DIY Wildflower Wedding Experience

I have always been captivated by weddings. I'm not talking about those over-the-top bridezilla sort of weddings where the bride has a hissy fit because 5,000 rare orchids haven't been flown in from Manila on time. I'm talking about joyful, heartfelt weddings where the beauty of a couple's love for one another truly shines through.

* * *

Ever since I created Canada's first pick-your-own flower farm, I have helped make wildflower wedding dreams come true. Watching brides and their friends and family explore my wildflower fields for the first time is always an exciting experience for me. I know, too, that it is for them. At my farm, brides learn to play with the colors, textures and shapes of wildflowers and native grasses and to bring their floral visions to life.

Dreaming of your own DIY wildflower wedding? In a moment I will introduce you to the brides who collaborated with me to produce the three wildflower weddings featured in this book. These three women have widely differing personalities and lifestyles, but they share three qualities that are essential for a successful DIY wedding:

Flexibility! Nature and weather will always factor into what is available the day you pick your wedding flowers. You must be willing to embrace what Mother Nature provides.

Open-mindedness! A vivid imagination and passion for learning will allow you to get the most out of the wildflower treasures available to you.

A love of nature! This goes without saying. You wouldn't want a wildflower wedding if you didn't already have an appreciation for nature. Creating a wildflower bouquet can be just a relaxing wander through the garden and picking a few pretty blossoms. Or it can be a true collaboration with nature herself – and a reflection of her intricate beauty.

The Wildflower Farm Wedding Process

Here's how it works: To begin, the bride and I correspond by email or chat on the phone. Then, we meet at my farm to discuss her wedding plans; as she reviews her wedding plans I listen carefully; I take note of the number of guests, the number of bridesmaids, the number of groomsmen, where the wedding and reception will take place. When I inquire what sort of bridal bouquet she has in mind, suddenly, her face softens and her eyes light up. The discussion quickly becomes a rapid fire exchange of color preferences, favorite flowers and bouquet styles. A collaboration has been sparked that continues by phone and email right up until we reconvene at the farm two weeks prior to the wedding. It's time to make her floral vision a reality.

We wander the gardens, buckets and clippers in hand, the bride gleefully choosing every beautiful wildflower and native grass that reflects her wedding style. Then, together she and I build the bridal bouquet of her dreams. Once we have mastered the bridal bouquet it's a breeze to build samples of the bridesmaid's bouquet, the boutonnieres and the table arrangements.

One Week and Counting! A week or so before the wedding, the bride and her design team visit the farm for a wedding design intensive. They will depart three hours later, knowing how to efficiently and confidently fashion every boutonniere, bouquet and table arrangement to the bride's specifications.

One day and counting! On harvesting day the bride and her team arrive early in the morning with many buckets. After several hours of harvesting, the bride and her posse whisk the flowers away to a cool location, where the flowers are stored overnight.

Wedding bells will chime! The bride's make-shift design studio lovingly churns out magnificent table arrangements, boutonnieres, bridal bouquets and the pièce de résistance: a stunning wildflower bridal bouquet!

Our Three Brides

Now, let's meet our brides, Chantelle, Katrina and Anne, and share some gorgeous photos of each one's "day of days." There's something magical about a wildflower wedding!

Chantelle ❧

July 6, 2013
Theme: *Country, Rustic, Vintage*
145 guests
Wedding at small, country church
Reception at parents' cattle farm

Chantelle's bouquet was a cascading combination of native and non-native flowers.

Each pew of the church was decorated with small wildflower displays held in mason jars filled with water to keep them fresh.

The table arrangements were filled with a combination of native and non-native flowers placed in large galvanized buckets.

"I didn't participate in the final floral designs. My sister, Renee, headed the design team." - *Chantelle*

Katrina

August 3, 2013
Theme: *Romantic, Shabby Chic, Do-It-Yourself*
100 guests
Wedding and reception at rural outdoor
education and recreation center

Katrina's bridesmaids loved their bouquets!

The base of Katrina's wildflower bouquet was Wild
Quinine with some Rattlesnake Master and 'Silver King'
Artemisia into which she added White Cohosh for
height and Nodding Wild Onion for color.

An elegant welcome
for an elegant
wedding.

I loved that the flowergirl baskets were
so bright and funky.

Anne ☙

August 24, 2013
Theme: *A Grownup Fair*
120 guests
Wedding and reception at rural fairgrounds

"We wanted a wedding that wasn't pompous or uptight."
– *Anne*

"It was easy to expand that design mojo I had going when it came to the reception tables. They looked kind of empty, so I added some crayons." - *Esther, one of Anne's bridesmaids.*

Each bridesmaid showcased her individual style in her choice of dress and bouquet design.

Anne and Nick had Blue False Indigo pods available to the guests. The guests held up their natural maracas to congratulate the new couple.

After all the excitement of the weddings had calmed down and everyone had returned to their normal lives again, I arranged "debriefing" sessions with the new brides and members of their wedding parties about their experiences. I asked lots of questions: What were their favorite wildflowers? What were their best memories and what were the challenges? And much more. A typical comment came from Anne's new husband, Nick, who said, "We became more involved than I could have imagined, but with good reason. It was a lot of work, but totally worth it! Our guests kept telling us the flowers made it the most aesthetically beautiful wedding they'd ever seen." You can see the complete debriefings on our website, www.tamingwildflowers.com.

Your DIY Wildflower Wedding Flowers

Now that you've seen the beauty and vibrancy that wildflowers lend to weddings, especially when they are handled with such care and affection, you can learn how to build your own wildflower wedding, from bouquets to boutonnieres. As you work through the projects below, remember that the most important thing is to make these arrangements your own. Choose what speaks to you and you will surely create your perfect DIY wildflower wedding.

Let's get designing!

Bridal Bouquet

The bridal bouquet and those made for the bridesmaids are similar except that the bridal bouquet will be larger and often more colorful.

Design Supplies

Floral tape, floral picks, floral wire, fabric for wrapping bridal bouquet stems, fresh floral foam, scissors

Set up your design space with access to all of your supplies to make bouquet production quick and easy.

Now, Do It Yourself!

1. Choose flat-headed or umbel-shaped flowers and gradually work the blooms into a dome shape that is slightly higher in the middle and gradually tapers downward.

Anne used Wild Quinine as the base of her bouquet.

Wiggle the stems through the base to add more flowers. Loosen your grip and pull the stem from the bottom to the desired height.

2. Choose a primary design element, either a spike or daisy-shaped flower.
3. Loosen your grip on the stems just enough to carefully plunge the primary design stem down into the dome. For daisy shapes, the circle remains above the background dome. For spires, you decide how far you want the spike to stick up above the dome.
4. Insert an odd number of stems in a pleasing pattern around the dome. Odd numbers create a more natural-looking bouquet. Choose another primary design element and repeat the process until you are satisfied.
5. If you are adding a foliage surround to the bouquet, simply encircle the flower dome with the foliage.

Keep adding to the bouquet until you think it's finished. Turn the bouquet to see it from all angles.

9. Cut off a 4-foot (1.2m) length of floral tape and wrap it tightly around the stems for a minimum of 3-inch (8cm) width to secure the stems.

Large leaves and other foliage can be added around a bouquet to add color, fullness or new textures.

10. Use corsage pins to secure fabric to the stems, then wrap the stems with the fabric. Fold the fabric under smoothly and use corsage pins to secure it.

11. Place your bouquet in a deep vase of water to keep it fresh until you need it.

6. Take a 2½- or 3-foot (80-90 cm) length of floral wire and make a small hook on one end. Gently hook an outside stem under the very top of the bouquet at the top of the stems. Then circle the wire around the stems at the top of the bouquet, pulling tightly as you go. This will stabilize the bouquet.

7. To lock your wiring, create another hook on the end of the wire and hook it around a stem. Manipulate the wire to flatten it high up under the neck of the dome to make sure it is secure and does not show. If you wish to bring the flowers in the dome closer together, simply push the wire as high as it will go up under the dome.

8. Cut the stems to a uniform length.

Katrina's final bouquet complete with Nodding Wild Onion, Wild Quinine, White Cohosh spikes, Joe-Pye Weed and some 'Silver King' Artemisia.

Boutonnières

Lovely boutonnieres artfully lined up on white plate all with curly tails like sea horses

Design Supplies

Flowers and leaves, floral tape and corsage pins, scissors

Now, Do It Yourself!

1. Choose a background material such as a broad, shiny leaf or a background flower.
2. Choose one or two small primary design materials.
3. Carefully fashion a very small fan from the primary design elements you have chosen. Center this overtop of the background material.
4. Cut the stems to an even length.
5. Wind floral tape around the stems.
6. Use a corsage pin to adhere the leaf or background flower to the gentlemen's lapels

Flower Girl Basket

Design Supplies
Flowers, a small basket with handle, plastic liner, floral foam for fresh flowers or dried flower foam for dried flowers; ribbon, scissors, and knife

Now Do It Yourself!
1. If you are using fresh flowers, submerge a floral foam brick into a bucket of water. Use a weight to keep it from bobbing up or use your hand to hold it down. Let the floral foam soak until it is fully saturated and heavy.

2. Line the basket with thick plastic liner to prevent water from leaking. A garbage bag will work just fine.
3. Place the wet floral foam into the plastic liner of the basket, using a knife to cut the foam to size. Make sure the foam fits snugly and isn't wobbling around.
4. Cut some foliage, varying the stem length between 3 and 6 inches (7-15 cm), and insert into the foam brick. Position the foliage around the edge of the basket and some in the interior of the basket.

5. Trim flower stems down to varying lengths between 3 and 6 inches (7-15 cm). Then place the flowers at varying depths until the basket looks full and lush.
6. Using a 2-foot (60 cm) length of ribbon, tie the ribbon in a simple bow around the handle of the basket.

Wedding Table Arrangements

Wedding table arrangements are very similar to making any flower arrangement; you simply have to design a large number of them in a short period of time (refer to the instructions in Chapter 7).

Well there you have it! Three very amazing women and three dramatically different DIY wildflower weddings. I enjoyed collaborating with these awe-inspiring women because each one possesses an open-mindedness, an ability to trust in her unique creative process and a passion for nature. How joyful for each woman to share these floriferous expressions of her inner being with her family, friends and new partner in life! Weddings are, of course, a celebration of life. And, what better flowers to participate in a celebration of life than those flowers that masterfully and beautifully support life on our glorious planet – the wildflowers. 🌼

Each bride had a different wedding style and each of them did an exceptional job in customizing their table arrangements.

WEDDING ALBUM – DESIGN WORKSHOP

WEDDING ALBUM – CHANTELLE

July 6, 2013

WEDDING ALBUM – KATRINA

WEDDING ALBUM – ANNE

Last Words

The genesis of this book sprang from my ongoing passion for wildflowers and my belief that wildflowers have a place in any and all gardens and bouquets. I am humbled by their beauty and by the essential services they provide to our pollinators and our planet. It is my fervent wish that I have inspired you to grow wildflowers in your landscape and to proudly display wildflowers in your favorite vase.

The selected bibliography and a resource guide for all the material used in this book can be found online. There, you will also find additional wildflower and wedding images, design instruction, wildflower growing information, the Wildflower Farm and *Taming Wildflowers* blog and a community of like-minded wildflower lovers. It is my hope that you'll find the site to be an informative aid and an entertaining annotation to *Taming Wildflowers*.

To access this information please go to: www.tamingwildflowers.com

Index – Wildflowers and Native Grasses

Beardtongue – *Penstemon grandiflorus* 5, 41, 42

Bergamot, Beebalm – *Monarda fistulosa* 60

Black–Eyed Susan – *Rudbeckia hirta* 50, 55, 56, 149, 150, 152

Blanketflower – *Gaillardia aristata* 43, 149, 150, 154

Blue False Indigo, Wild Blue Indigo – *Baptisia australis* 48, 49, 148, 155

Blue Flax, Wild Blue Flax – *Linum lewisii* 44, 149, 150

Blue Vervain – *Verbena hastata* 61, 155

Butterflyweed, Butterfly Milkweed – *Asclepias tuberosa* 50, 78, 152, 155

Cardinal Flower – *Lobelia cardinalis* 16, 62, 66

Common Evening Primrose – *Oenothera biennis* 21, 63

Common Milkweed – *Asclepias syriaca* 79

Compass Plant – *Silphium laciniatum* 88, 164

Culver's Root – *Veronicastrum virginicum* 64, 155

Cup Plant – *Silphium perfoliatum* 89, 90

Dotted Mint, Spotted Beebalm – *Monarda punctata* 65

Downy Sunflower – *Helianthus mollis* 96

Golden Alexanders – *Zizia aurea* 34

Great Blue Lobelia – *Lobelia siphilitica* 66, 155

Harebell – *Campanula rotundifolia* 41, 45

Hoary Vervain – *Verbena stricta* 67, 163, 164

Ironweed – *Vernonia fasciculata* 16, 99, 68

Lance Leaf Coreopsis, Sand Coreopsis – *Coreopsis lanceolata* 46

Lavender Hyssop, Licorice Hyssop – *Agastache foeniculum* 69, 153, 164

Meadow Blazingstar – *Liatris ligulistylis* 92, 148, 149, 155

Mountain Mint – *Pycnanthemum virginianum* 70, 152

New England Aster – *Symphyotrichum novae-angliae* 100, 164

Nodding Wild Onion – *Allium cernuum* 71, 174, 178

Ox–Eye Sunflower, False Sunflower – *Heliopsis helianthoides* 97, 149

Ozark Coneflower – *Echinacea paradoxa* 82

Pale Purple Coneflower – *Echinacea pallida* 83, 149, 152

Pasque Flower – *Anemone patens* 35

Prairie Blazingstar – *Liatris pycnostachya* 93, 149, 151

Prairie Dock; Prairie Rosinweed – *Silphium terebinthinaceum* 90

Prairie Smoke – *Geum triflorum* 36, 155, 164

Purple Coneflower – *Echinacea purpurea* 84, 164

Purple Prairie Clover – *Dalea purpurea* 48, 50, 148, 149, 150

Rattlesnake Master – *Eryngium yuccifolium* 72, 149, 151, 152, 155, 174

Red Milkweed, Swamp Milkweed – *Asclepias incarnata* 80, 155, 163

Rough Blazingstar – *Liatris aspera* 92, 94, 164

Shooting Star – *Dodecatheon meadia* 34, 37, 155

Showy Goldenrod – *Solidago speciosa* 101, 103, 155

Silver Sage, Silver King – *Artemisia ludoviciana* 73, 174, 178

Sky Blue Aster – *Symphyotrichum oolentangiense* 102, 149

Smooth Solomon's Seal – *Polygonatum biflorum* 38

Spiderwort – *Tradescantia ohiensis* 41, 47, 152

Stiff Goldenrod – *Oligoneuron rigidum* 103

Sweet Black–Eyed Susan – *Rudbeckia subtomentosa* 57

Sweet Joe–Pye Weed – *Eupatorium purpureum* 74, 178

Tennessee Coneflower – *Echinacea tennesseensis* 30, 85

White False Indigo, Wild White Indigo – *Baptisia alba* 48, 51, 155

White Yarrow – *Achillea millefolium* 75, 150, 164

Wild Columbine, Eastern Columbine – *Aquilegia canadensis* 39

Wild Lupine, Sundial Lupine – *Lupinus perennis* 34, 48, 52

Wild Quinine – *Parthenium integrifolium* 76, 152, 155, 164, 174, 177, 178

Wild Senna – *Senna hebecarpa* 48, 53, 155

Yellow Coneflower, Gray–Head Coneflower – *Ratibida pinnata* 86, 148, 151

Yellow False Indigo – *Baptisia sphaerocarpa* 54

Grasses:

Big Bluestem – *Andropogon gerardii* 104, 152, 155

Little Bluestem – *Schizachyrium scoparium* 152, 155, 164

Prairie Dropseed – *Sporobolus heterolepis* 105, 149, 152

* * *

Non–Profiled Plants Mentioned or Pictured in the Book

Bottlebrush Grass – *Elymus hystrix*

Branched Coneflower; Brown–Eyed Susan – *Rudbeckia triloba*

Canada Wild Rye – *Elymus canadensis*

Green–Headed Coneflower – *Rudbeckia laciniata*

Hairy Penstemon – *Penstemon hirsutus*

Indiangrass – *Sorghastrum nutans*

Northern Sea Oats – *Chasmanthium latifolium*

Dark–Throat Shooting Star – *Dodecatheon pulchellum*

Side Oats Grama – *Bouteloua curtipendula*

Smooth Aster – *Symphyotrichum laeve*

Smooth Penstemon – *Penstemon digitalis*

Switch Grass – *Panicum virgatum*

Virginia Bluebells – *Mertensia virginica*

White Aster – *Oligoneuron album*

Wine Cups – *Calliroe involucrate, Calliroe digitata, Calliroe bushiii*

Best Wildflowers/Native Grasses by Soil Type

I. CLAY

Flowers:

Beebalm – *Monarda fistulosa*
Black-Eyed Susan – *Rudbeckia hirta*
Blue Vervain – *Verbena hastate*
Columbine – *Aquilegia canadensis*
Common Milkweed – *Asclepias syriaca*
Compass Plant – *Silphium laciniatum*
Coreopsis – *Coreopsis lanceolata*
Culver's Root – *Veronicum virginicum*
Cup Plant – *Silphium perfoliatum*
Golden Alexanders – *Zizia aurea*
Great Blue Lobelia – *Lobelia syphilitica*
Maximilian Sunflower – *Heliathus maximilliani*
New England Aster – *Symphyotrichum novae-angilae*
Ox-Eye Sunflower – *Heliopsis helianthoides*
Ozark Coneflower – *Echinacea paradoxa*
Pale Purple Coneflower – *Echincea pallida*
Prairie Blazingstar – *Liatris pychnostachya*
Prairie Dock - *Silphium terebinthinaceum*
Purple Coneflower – *Echinacea Purpurea*
Purple Prairie Clover – *Dalea purpurea*
Rattlesnake Master – *Eryngium yuccifolium*
Red Milkweed – *Asclepias incarnate*
Spiderwort – *Tradescantia ohiensis*
Stiff Goldenrod – *Solidago rigida*
Sweet Black Eyed Susan – *Rudbeckia subtomentosa*
Sweet Joe-Pye Weed – *Eurpatorium purpureum*
Wild Quinine – *Parthenium integrifolium*
Wild Senna – *Senna hebecarpa*
Yellow Coneflower – *Ratibida pinnata*

Grasses:

Big Bluestem – *Andropogon gerardii*
Indiangrass – *Sorghastrum nutans*
Little Bluestem – *Schizachyrium scoparium*
Northern Sea Oats – *Chasmanthium latifolium*

II. SANDY, DRY SOIL

Flowers:

Beardtongue – *Penstemon grandiflora*
Beebalm – *Monarda fistulosa*
Black-Eyed Susan – *Rudbeckia hirta*
Blanketflower – *Gaillardia aristata*
Blue False Indigo – *Baptisia australis*
Blue Flax – *Linum lewisii*
Butterflyweed – *Asclepias tuberosa*
Native Columbine – *Aquilegia canadensis*
Compass Plant – *Silphium laciniatum*
Culver's Root – *Veronicum virginicum*
Cup Plant – *Sylphium perfoliatum*
Dotted Mint – *Monarda punctate*
Downy Sunflower – *Helianthus mollis*
Evening Primrose – *Oenothera biennis*
Golden Alexanders – *Zizia aurea*
Green Headed Coneflower – *Rudbeckia laciniata*
Harebell – *Campanula rotundifolia*
Maximilian's Sunflower – *Heliathus maximilliani*
Hoary Vervain – *Verbena stricta*
Lanceleaf Coreopsis – *Coreopsis lanceolata*
Lavender hyssop – *Agastache foeniculatum*
Mountain Mint – *Pycnanthemum*

Native Lupine – *Lupinus perennis*
New England Aster – *Symphyotrichum novae-angliae*
Nodding Wild Onion – *Allium cernuum*
Ox-Eye Sunflower – *Heliopsis helianthoides*
Ozark Coneflower – *Echinacea paradoxa*
Pale Purple Coneflower – *Echinacea pallida*
Pasque Flower – *Anemone patens*
Prairie Blazingstar – *Liatris pychnostachya*
Prairie Dock – *Silphium terebinthinaceum*
Prairie Smoke – *Geum triflorum*
Purple Coneflower – *Echinacea purpurea*
Purple Prairie Clover – *Dalea purpurea*
Rattlesnake Master – *Eryngium yuccifolium*
Rough Blazingstar – *Liatris aspera*
Showy Goldenrod – *Solidago speciosa*
Side Oats Grama – *Bouteloua curtipendula*
Sky Blue Aster – *Symphyotrichum oolentangiense*
Smooth Penstemon – *Penstemon digitalis*
Stiff Goldenrod – *Soligado rigida*
Sweet Black-Eyed Susan – *Rudbeckia subtomentosa*
Tennessee Coneflower – *Echinacea tennesseensis*
White Aster – *Oligoneuron album*
White False Indigo – *Baptisia alba*
White Yarrow – *Achillia millifolium*
Wild Quinine – *Parthenium integrifolium*
Wild Senna – *Senna hebecarpa*
Yellow Coneflower – *Ratibida pinnata*
Yellow False Indigo – *Baptisia sphaerocarpa*

Best Wildflowers/Native Grasses by Soil Type

Grasses:

Big Bluestem – *Andropogon gerardii*
Little Bluestem – *Schizachyrium scoparium*
Prairie Dropseed – *Sporobolus heterolepsis*
Switch Grass – *Panicum virgatum*

III. LOAM

Flowers:

Artemesia – *Artemesia ludoviciana*
Beebalm – *Monarda fistulosa*
Black-Eyed Susan – *Rudbeckia hirta*
Blanketflower – *Gaillardia arista*
Blue False Indigo – *Baptisia australis*
Blue Flax – *Linum lewisii*
Blue Vervain – *Verbena hastate*
Branched Coneflower – *Rudbeckia triloba*
Butterflyweed – *Asclepias tuberosa*
Cardinal Flower – *Lobelia cardinalis*
Common Milkweed – *Asclepias syriaca*
Compass Plant – *Silphium laciniatum*
Culver's Root – *Virginium veronicastrum*
Cup Plant – *Silphium perfoliatum*
Dotted Mint – *Monarda punctate*
Downy Sunflower – *Helianthus mollis*
Evening Primrose – *Oenothera biennis*
Foam Flower – *Tiarella cordifolia*
Golden Alexanders – *Zizia aurea*
Great Blue Lobelia – *Lobelia syphilitica*
Green Headed Coneflower – *Rudbecia laciniata*
Harebell – *Campanula rotundifolia*
Hoary Vervain – *Verbena stricta*
Ironweed – *Vernonia fasciculate*
Jacob's Ladder – *Polemonium reptans*

Lanceleaf Coreopsis – *Coreopsis lanceolata*
Lavender Hyssop – *Agastache foeniculum*
Meadow Blazingstar – *Liatris ligulistylus*
Mountain Mint – *Pyracanthum virginianum*
Native Columbine – *Aquilegia canadensis*
Native Lupine – *Lupine perennis*
New England Aster – *Symphyotrichum novae-angliae*
Nodding Wild Onion – *Allium cernuum*
Ozark Coneflower – *Echinacea paradoxa*
Pale Purple Coneflower – *Ecinacea pallida*
Pasque Flower – *Anemone patens*
Prairie Blazingstar – *Liatris pychnostachya*
Prairie Dock – *Silphium terebinthinaceum*
Prairie Smoke – *Geum triflorum*
Purple Prairie Clover – *Dalea purpureum*
Rattlesnake Master – *Eryngium yuccifolium*
Red Milkweed – *Asclepias incarnate*
Rough Blazingstar – *Liatris aspera*
Shooting Star – *Dodecatheon meadia*
Showy Goldenrod – *Solidago speciosa*
Sky Blue Aster – *Symphyotrichum oolentangiense*
Smooth Aster – *Symphyotrichum laeve*
Smooth Penstemon – *Penstemon digitalis*
Solomon Seal – *Polygonatum biflorum*
Spiderwort – *Tradescantia ohiensis*
Stiff Goldenrod – *Solidago rigida*
Sweet Black-eyed Susan – *Rudbeckia subtomentosa*
Sweet Joe-Pye Weed – *Eupatorium purpureum*
Tennessee Coneflower – *Echinacea tennesseensis*

Virginia Bluebells – *Mertensia virginiana*
Virginia Wild Rye – *Elymus virginicus*
White False Indigo – *Baptisia alba*
White Yarrow – *Achillia millifolium*
Wild Quinine – *Parthenium integrifolium*
Wild Senna – *Senna hebecarpa*
Yellow Coneflower – *Ratibida pinnata*
Yellow False Indigo – *Baptisia sphaerocarpa*

Grasses:

Big Bluestem – *Andropogon gerardii*
Canada Wild Rye – *Elymus canadensis*
Indiangrass – *Sorghastrum nutans*
Little Bluestem – *Schizichryum scoparium*
Northern Sea Oats – *Chasmanthium latifolium*
Prairie Dropseed – *Sporobolus heterolepsis*
Side Oats Grama – *Bouteloua curtipendula*
Switch Grass – *Panicum virgatum*

Acknowledgments

A special thank-you to the brides, their families and friends! We started out as strangers talking about flowers and ended up sharing wonderful memories.

Thank you to workshop, wedding and tattoo photographers – Nikki Heseltine, Emilie Santi and Courtney-Lee Yip, Maria Levertov, Teri Dunn and Natasha McFayden. I am indebted to Yvonne Cunnnington for her stunning meadow photography. Thanks to Wendy Hutchinson of Studio Wendy for lending me her gorgeous Raku pottery.

I am grateful to esteemed Canadian colleagues for your support over these many years – Helen and Sarah Battersby, Mark Cullen, Yvonne Cunnington, Janet Davis, Lorraine Flannigan, Theresa Forte, Beckie Fox, Nikki Jabbour, Marjorie Harris, Jeff Mason, Rona and Fredelle Maynard, Ellen Novack, Tony Spencer and the peerless Paul Zammit.

Thanks to cherished colleagues of the plant scribe tribe; Kylee Baumle, Kevin Braag, Karen Chapman, Susan Cohan, Shawna Coronado, Evelyn Hadden, Annie Haven , LaManda Joy, Liz Licata, Laura Livengood, Sharon Lovejoy, Laura Matthews, Kerry Michaels, Susan Morrison, Teresa O'Conner, Riz Reyes, Cristina Salwitz, Aldona Satterthwaite, Fran Sorin, Amanda Thompson, James Trudy Verell, Linda Wesson and Helen Yoest.

A huge thank-you to Duncan Brine, Marielle Anzelone and Dana Buzzeli for allowing me to share your passion for wildflowers. I have learned so much from Native Plant educators: Anne Bossart, Carole Sevilla Brown, Thomas Christopher, Neil Diboll, Susan Dingwell, Gail Eichenberg, Chris Kreussling, Lorraine Johnson, Noel Kingsbury, Janet Marinelli, Beatriz Moisset, , Ginny Sibolt, Susan J. Tweit, Kelly Senser, Vincent Vizachero, Benjamin Vogt, Sally and Andy Wasowski and Catherine Zimmerman.

A heartfelt thank-you to the Specialty Cut Flower Growers Association. And a special thanks to Debra Prinzing for encouraging me to write about this floriferous life. Long overdue thanks to Mark and the late Terry Silber for their everlasting inspiration.

Along the way I've received incalculable support from: Louise Cohen, the late Pete Cook and Annie Wysor Graham, Bernadette Hardacre, Ruth Kahn, Kalli Kronmiller, Tina May Luker, Kate Crane McCarthy, Tom Morrissey, Jackie Polland, John Rabinowitz, Erica Ross, Raffaela Tassone , Nicola Warnock and Nancy Wells.

Thanks to Jack and Kim Campbell who lent two cityots their bright orange tractor until the cityots got their own green one.

Acknowledgments

Thanks to soulful dance mentor Julie Leavitt, for helping me rediscover the true meaning of my wildflower home.

An extra special thanks to floral designer extraordinaire Sherry Smith, the Gingerbread Lady, who took me under her wing, selflessly sharing design and life lessons with me.

Thanks to wise and wonderful family elders Len and Harriet Kronman, and Sol and Charlotte Masters, for a lifetime of advice, love and support. And a huge thank you to brothers Paul and Joe for being the warm, witty and talented men that they are and continuing to share the love.

I am indebted to my fully-grown offspring Keith, Elias and Nora, who have always been intelligent, loving and admirable human beings despite the traumas they endured growing up with a florally-obsessed mother.

I cherish the support of Ellen Kolba and Ellen Walters Sousa who never wavered in their belief in me as a writer.

Thanks to my father, Morris Goldberger, publisher, editor and sage, for patiently teaching me to write. It was Moe who urged me to tell my story and gave me the book that inspired me: "How Flowers Changed the World," by Loren Eiseley. Thanks to my mother, Edna Goldberger, for being the fiercely flamboyant lover of beauty that she was.

Thanks to Marette Sharp for her outstanding efforts to ensure the timely delivery of *Taming Wildflowers* to St. Lynn's Press.

Tremendous thanks to Paul Kelly, publisher, St. Lynn's Press, for giving this new author the opportunity to speak her mind and heart; to editor Cathy Dees, who supports the birth of books like a seasoned midwife, offering just the right balance of encouragement and structure; to designer Holly Rosborough, for designing a beautiful book that puts the beauty of wildflowers front and center.

About the Author

Long before "green" or "sustainable" became the powerful buzzwords they are today, Miriam Goldberger began growing wildflowers – falling madly in love with the beauty and practicality that native plants bring to our lives. A flower farmer since 1986, Miriam has seeded, planted, nurtured, harvested and created floral designs with thousands upon thousands of wildflowers. As an expert in organic and sustainable gardening, Miriam is on intimate terms with the easy steps gardeners and flower lovers can take to create beautiful, diverse and sustainable landscapes. She is the founder and co-owner of Wildflower Farm, a wildflower seed production company in Ontario, Canada; a magical 100 acres where the wildflower gardens and meadows thrive without irrigation or pesticides – a pollinators' paradise. To see Miriam among her wildflowers is to truly see a woman outstanding in her field.

www.tamingwildflowers.com • www.wildflowerfarm.com